MEDIA MANUALS

Local Radio

PRINTED IN CANADA

D1178713

MEDIA MANUALS

Local Radio

DATE DUE

Barrie Redfern

Focal Press · London

Focal/Hastings House · New York

🔲🔲 **British Library Cataloguing in Publication Data**

Redfern, Barrie
  Local radio. – (Media manuals).
  1. Radio broadcasting
  I. Title   II. Series
621.3841'64   PN1991.5

ISBN (excl. USA) 0 240 50980 3
ISBN (USA only) 0 8038 4311 9

Printed in Great Britain by A. Wheaton & Co. Ltd., Exeter

Contents

Introduction

Local radio stations have professional and extremely dedicated groups of staff able to perform a variety of jobs ranging from announcing, reporting and tape editing to producing programmes. Although they do broadcast, they also rely to a great extent on freelances and contributors for expert knowledge and comment. These people are not on staff but may, in the case of sports reporters, earn their living from journalism. Other contributors have jobs outside the media and broadcast because of their expert knowledge of a particular subject—gardening, jazz, folk music, religion, sport, science, etc. The work varies considerably from station to station. In some areas you may be asked to read a short voice piece whilst in others it may well mean producing or presenting a specialist programme. British local radio is unique in that many of its programmes (including those from the smaller community stations on cable systems) are made or compiled by local radio.

All programmes are either made or supervised by staff personnel who, although able to offer advice and guidance, do expect a minimum of broadcasting standards. This book is intended to provide an insight into local radio—whether you are an avid listener or feel you have something to offer your local studios. Useful advice is also included for clubs, societies, and organizations seeking publicity for their events.

The job of DJ is probably one of the most sought after in radio. Just as with the press journalist and his radio counterpart there are similarities between the role of the discotheque DJ and the radio DJ—but with a whole new world of technical skills. Advice is given about all the ancillary jobs a radio DJ frequently has to do. From the smallest of the community stations working from single studios to specialist stations and those covering whole counties this book explains the basic techniques used in local radio.

Broadcast Chain

Local radio stations basically consist of a production area with one or more studios and control rooms, newsroom, production offices, and workshop. Studios and control rooms are linked to a master control room where programmes are switched and monitored before being fed to the transmitters. The master control room (MCR) is in effect the centre of operations (the name 'operations room' is used at some stations) though individual studio control rooms act as the MCR when there is only one studio.

Most control desks (also known as boards or panels), for both studio and master control, can accommodate a number of sources linked to the mixer, including record turntables, tape recorders, microphones, outside lines and radio links.

Programmes

Throughout the day hundreds of operations are performed on the control board to bring in the different sources at the right times. Contributions may come from various other studios, police and weather stations, sports stadia, network, and listeners themselves (e.g. by telephone). Items may be received either recorded on tape or live by telephone, land line, or radio link, e.g. radio car. Most stations have a radio car or mobile units for transmitting programme inserts back to base. Usually one or more receiving aerials (antennae) are installed on high buildings and linked by music line (see p. 14) to the studios. Programmes often include telephone inserts e.g. phone-ins, in this case special lines and a switchboard are allocated thus keeping other phone lines free for normal office use. Information can also be sent via a teleprinter from national newsrooms or agencies, weather and police stations etc. National news sent by teleprinter allows local stations to broadcast the news in their own style, and also means the local implications of the story can be given.

Control

Programmes are mixed on a control board situated either in a studio (with the presenter operating the programme) or small control cubicle. From there, the programme, which may consist of many inserts e.g. voice from studio, tape inserts, discs etc., is fed either to a tape recorder (if it is to be transmitted later) or to the MCR which may also be the same studio (see p. 52). There the programme is monitored for technical quality and, sometimes, other items inserted e.g. commercials. Finally, the programme is routed to the transmitters or relay service via high quality land lines.

OUTGOING LINES

Music lines carry the programme to the transmitters and relay service. They also link the station to news contribution circuits.

Control lines provide cue and talkback to remote studios etc.

A station may have several lines between studio centre and telephone exchange with some sources e.g. transmitters and programme feeds permanently wired, and the rest plugged up as required.

Internal lines link the MCR to the apparatus room.

Sources feeding the MCR and studio.

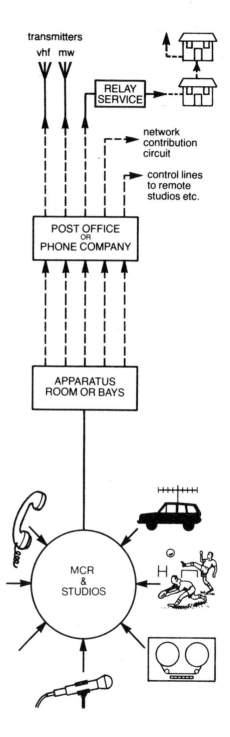

transmitters
vhf mw

RELAY SERVICE

network contribution circuit

control lines to remote studios etc.

POST OFFICE
OR
PHONE COMPANY

APPARATUS ROOM OR BAYS

MCR
&
STUDIOS

11

Studio and Recording Discipline

Production areas are acoustically treated to control the amount of reflected sound and also to prevent noise from elsewhere breaking through and being picked up by microphones. Windows between studios and control rooms are double glazed (those looking out of the building may be triple glazed) and double doors with rubber seals lead into the studio. Floors are carpeted on a layer of felt, and walls fitted with sound absorbers. The ceiling is also acoustically treated, usually with special tiles.

Furniture is carefully selected or constructed to avoid sound reflections. Most chairs and table tops have fabric covers. Some talk tables are transparent to sound, having a perforated metal surface covered in fabric.

Loudspeakers and red lights

Studio loudspeakers are arranged to cut whenever a microphone fader is opened and red lights operated. If this did not happen the sound from the loudspeaker would be picked up by the microphone, amplified and fed through the loudspeaker again, the whole process very quickly building up to an intolerable feedback. Headphones are used for monitoring in a live studio.

Occasionally information has to be taken into a live studio e.g. a news flash, in which case any control room or nearby loudspeaker has to be switched off (cut) and the door opened slowly and as little as possible. Red lights above studio doors indicate when the studio is live.

Noises

Thick paper is used in single sheets for scripts with paper clips removed. Pages are lifted to one side in single sheets. Any noise made near to the microphone appears out of all proportion to the listener and quite likely to sound completely different. Common noise problems are lighting cigarettes, clicking of ballpoint pens, and the rattle of jewellery. Pouring of drinks is best carried out before entering the studio and certainly ring-pull cans should never be opened on air.

Some clothing even makes a noise, especially when rubbed along the desk top. People who are likely to cough or sneeze very heavily should be politely asked to turn their head away from the microphone to do so—in the same way as one would not sneeze in front of someone's face. Guests, though, should never be afraid to clear their throats on air. People who desperately plough on often sound as though they are being strangled. In a recording session pieces can be taken again and any coughs etc., cut out afterwards.

When recording in an interviewee's home always look out for troublesome noise spots, a ticking clock, dogs, telephones, etc.

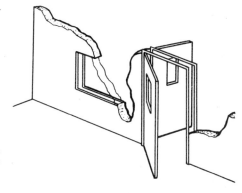

The studio
Studio windows are double glazed.
Double doors link studios and con-
trol rooms with other areas.

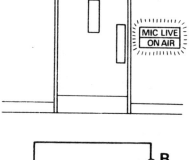

Red light
Live studios have glowing or flashing red lights near the studio and
control room doors.

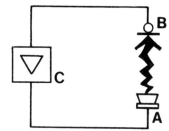

Loudspeaker cut
Feedback occurs when sound from
the loudspeaker (A) is picked up by
the microphone (B) and transferred
to the amplifier (C) and amplified
over and over again.

Noise
Very often the smallest things can
create most trouble e.g. the clicking
of pens.

Scripts
Stiff paper is used and turned up at
the edges to help move pages si-
lently.

Lines

Lines are used for linking remote studios, transmitters, networks, other radio stations, and outside broadcasts to the studio centre. Distortion occurs in all land lines, resulting in a loss of level, particularly at the higher audio frequencies. Generally, the greater the distance is the greater the loss.

Attenuation and Equalization

An even frequency response can be restored to a line by using an equalizer, which smooths out remaining peaks in the frequency range. In effect, this reduces the overall signal level, so an amplifier is incorporated to restore the original level. Different lines suffer from varying degrees of attenuation at particular frequencies, so equalizers are designed to suit individual lines. Equalizers are usually inserted at the receiving end of a line, though a signal can be boosted at certain frequencies before being sent out to compensate for line losses. Stereo lines have to be specially matched to give similar characteristics.

Music and Control Lines

Lines used for programme purposes are equalized. High quality circuits with a good flat frequency response are called music lines because of their ability to carry music without impairing the quality, and they are used to carry programmes and contributions. They are also known as radio or program lines. Music lines such as those to the transmitters are permanently, hard, wired whilst others e.g. for outside broadcasts, are booked on a long or short-term basis.

Lower quality lines are used for providing programme cues to remote studios and sports stadia and are similar in quality to those used for the public telephone system. (In local radio ordinary telephone subscriber lines are sometimes used for cueing purposes.) These are called control or private lines. Alternatively, a music line can be used as a control line. Portable boxes for commentators can be fitted with switches for changing over equipment or lines. Control and music lines in and out of the station are usually terminated in a row of sockets in the apparatus or rack room from where they can be routed as required through the jackfield. From there, some lines are permanently linked to the studio control boards.

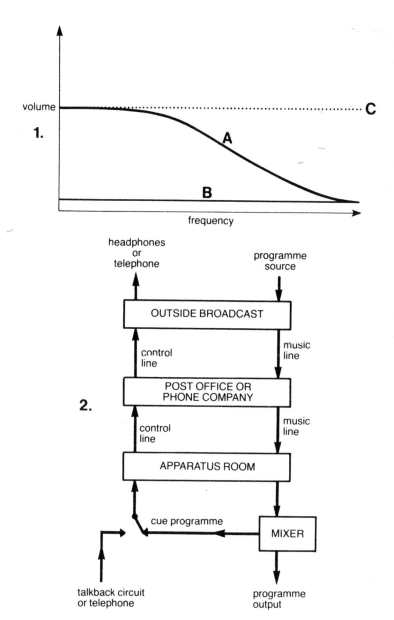

LINES
1. Equalizer. A, Signal suffering from high frequency loss in line. B, Signal after equalizer has attenuated all frequencies to a flat response. C, Amplifiers restore the level lost in the line and equalizer. 2. Example of use of control and music lines for an outside broadcast. Cue programme from the studio mixer or talkback can be switched to the control line. Talkback may either be from mixer talkback circuit or telephone.

Studio/Control Room

In local radio there is often very little difference between studios and control rooms. The control room is where sources are mixed to form complete programmes. Equipment normally includes at least two of all recording or reproducing equipment i.e. record turntables, tape recorders, and cartridge machines linked to a mixer. The output of the mixer desk is also fed to the recording machines so that programmes or inserts may be recorded as well as (or instead of) being transmitted live. The mixer is fitted into a desk including switches for monitoring and selecting sources, with the reproducing equipment grouped around the operator. The desk is also fitted with a talkback microphone and loudspeaker which act as an intercom to other production areas. Lines in and out of the mixer are routed through a jackfield or patch panel. A main jackfield for the whole station may be located in a separate apparatus or rack room though smaller panels may be allocated to each control room. Other equipment includes monitor loudspeakers, clocks, red transmission lights, and telephones (sometimes with a switchboard). The control room is also acoustically treated in the same way as the studio.

Studio

The studio, of course, is normally associated with microphones—the place where items are 'voiced'—the microphones being faded up or down from the control board. The traditional way of broadcasting was to have a producer and operator assemble a programme in the control room, and a presenter in a separate studio. In local radio, nowadays, these roles are blurred together—because programmes are mainly self-operated by the presenter, who is quite likely to be the producer as well. A broadcast quality microphone is simply added to the control board to turn it into a self-operational studio.

Normal studio conditions also have to be arranged for self-operational work i.e. loudspeaker cut when the microphones are opened, non-ringing telephones etc. This, therefore, makes for much more flexible working and increases the use of resources. Sometimes one room is designated as the control room, with a second mixer placed in another room for use as a self-operational studio. For complex programmes the control room mixer can be used, thus freeing the presenter to concentrate on links and continuity rather than operations. The control room may also be used as the master control room (or operations room) at some stations (see p. 52). Control of output to the transmitters may also be switched from one board to another. The actual facilities available vary from station to station.

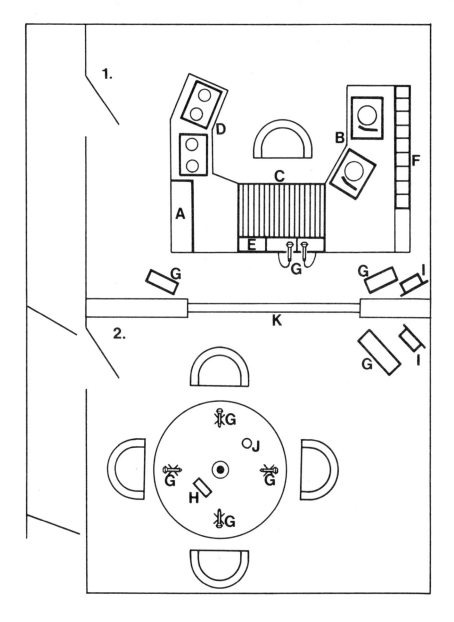

STUDIO CONTROL ROOM
Grouping of facilities
1. Control room or self-operational studio; 2, studio. All equipment is grouped around the operator for ease of control. A, Patch panel or jackfield; B, turntables; C, mixer and control panel; D, tape decks; E, cartridge machines; F, cartridge racks; G, microphones used separately or switched for programme and talkback purposes; H, Reverse talkback unit to the control room; I, clock and lamps (on air, rehearsal, and telephone lamps); J, cue light; K, double glazing.

Control Board

The control board or desk is made up of (a) the mixer; (b) switches for selecting sources where there are several, and routing the output to specific lines or groups; and (c) switches for cueing and monitoring.

The mixer is situated at waist level in front of the operator and may consist of a row of slider faders built into the working surface or an almost vertical panel of rotary faders. Rotary faders originate from the earliest days of broadcasting and though still used, occupy far more space than sliders which are smaller and easier to operate (with just one finger).

Faders are often arranged in groups, with those for the discs on the turntable side and those for tapes nearest the tape machines, with switchable and microphone faders in between. A master fader may be used to control the output of the mixer.

Input and output

On many multipurpose desks, certain faders may be switched to any one of a variety of sources thus increasing the immediate capabilities of the mixer. Multiway switches or an automatic switching matrix linked to the control board allow lines to be quickly selected and faded up without extra plugging on the jackfield. Studio facilities e.g. turntables, tape machines, etc., are wired via the jackfield to individual fader modules. The output of the mixer is routed through a switch for converting stereo output to mono if required, and fed to the master control room (if it is not originating the programme). The mixer output is also fed to the studio tape recorders so that programmes or inserts may be mixed and recorded instead of being broadcast live.

Other switches

Switches are arranged in groups according to their function. They include talkback, cue lights, limiter and compressor controls, remote controls for tape and cartridge machines, radio car control, etc. The output of other studios and networks can be selected on a ring main (multiway or rotary switch) which can, in turn, be switched to meters, loudspeakers and headphones for monitoring.

Other switches, when installed, are included for echo, grouping sources (sub-mixing), transmitter control and remote stereo switching of the transmitters.

The desk is also associated with ancillary equipment including telephones and switchboard, jackfield, and connectors for headphones etc.

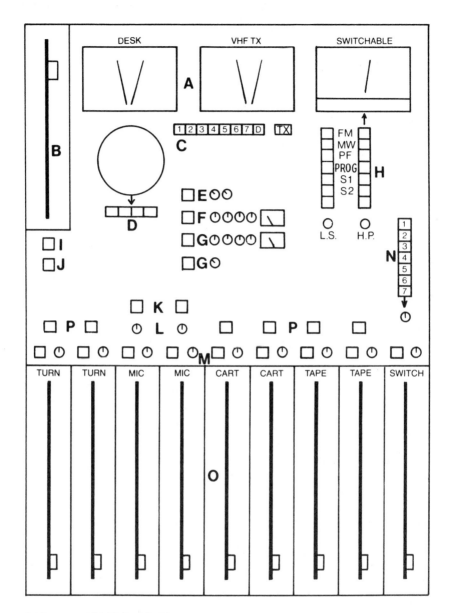

SIMPLIFIED CONTROL BOARD

Basic layout consists of A, meters for monitoring desk, transmission and other sources/outputs; B, master fader; C, transmitter control with buttons for switching sources including desk direct to transmitter, and also taking control; D, talkback to studios, radio car, etc.; E, switches for echo; F, limiters, G, voice-over unit, etc. (which may be located elsewhere); H, monitor or ring main switches for monitoring on meter, headphones and loudspeakers; I, stereo/pilot tone switch; J, mono/stereo output switch; K, cue light switches; L, pan pots; M, pre-fade and pre-set gain controls; N, multiway selector (or switching matrix) linked to miscellaneous fader; O, slider faders (usually opening away from operator); P, stop/start buttons.

Selecting Sources

When a whole range of outside sources are in daily use they are permanently (hard) wired to the mixer. Other lines and temporary feeds can be extended from the apparatus or rack room to the mixer as required.

Permanently wired lines
When only one or two lines are regularly used they may be allocated separate faders on the mixer. Stations with several lines e.g. remote studios, weather stations etc., have two or three faders on the mixer which can be plugged or switched to whichever source is required. The quickest and easiest method is to have all the regularly used lines routed to multi-way switches or a switching matrix on the control board with the outputs of the switches feeding separate faders. When two outside sources are needed, one after the other or together, one line is selected on one switch and fader, and the second line switched to on another fader.

Jackfield
The traditional way of selecting and routing sources is by patching or cross plugging. All the lines in and out of the mixers, tape machines etc., remote sources and even transmitters are routed through jackfields consisting of rows of sockets. 'Double enders' or 'patch cords' are short lengths of cable with plugs at each end and are used to interconnect the sockets. In this way remote sources which appear on the jackfield can be connected to spare channels on the mixer.

Several lines and equipment are permanently linked e.g. the output of the master control board is likely to be hard-wired to the transmitter feeds. Permanent connections though do still pass through the jackfield so that equipment can be removed or added without affecting programmes. The jack sockets act as switches. The connection between any two lines or equipment can be broken by inserting a jack plug in the appropriate socket. When the plug is inserted, contacts in the socket change over to the plug. Permanently wired lines and equipment can be quickly re-routed by inserting double enders between sockets. Two basic kinds of socket on the jackfield are break jacks which can be overplugged, and listen jacks which do not change over connections when plugs are inserted. Important break jacks which normally must never be disturbed are covered with red or black plastic buttons. Control staff are always consulted before using the jackfield.

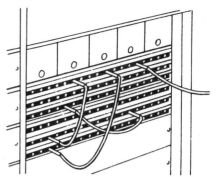

Jackfield
Panels for patching sources are located in most studios. Equipment and lines may be routed by linking appropriate jack sockets with double-enders.

Jackstrip and socket
Break jacks allow equipment to be cross-plugged. By inserting a jack plug the normal circuit is broken and the contacts changed over to the jack plug. Other types of arrangement allow plugs to be inserted without breaking the circuit.

Tuchel plug
In common use in Europe for cross-plugging.

Jack plug
Standard British Post Office design.

Double enders
Cables (of various lengths) with a plug at each end connect one socket to another.

Multiway switches
A single mixer module may be readily used for a variety of sources, when linked to a multiway switch on the board.

Audio switching matrix
A row of selector buttons on the control board are linked to electronic or electromechanical switches in the apparatus bays. The system also allows remote routing of output and accurate matching of lines with equipment

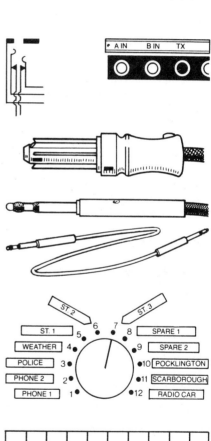

Fader Modules

The basic components of a fader module are the fader itself, a pre-fade (audition) key, and a pre-set control, together with a pan pot for stereo image. There are two basic types of fader used in local radio: sliders which are mounted either flat along the desk or inclined; and rotary ones which are mounted almost vertically. Slider faders are much narrower and therefore allow more to be fitted and controlled on one board. Sliders may be fitted either way round, the common international convention being to fade up away from the operator (though some organizations and studios do have the faders arranged the opposite way round). Rotary faders are opened clockwise and on studio boards have semi-circular plates attached to show how far the knob has been turned.

Channels
Most local radio mixers used for on-air work have two outputs. On stereo stations these form the left and right channels. Fader modules may be either for one or two channels. Single channel faders are allocated to microphones, outside broadcasts, and other mono sources. The output of single faders can be given a stereo position anywhere between left and right by using pan pots (short for panoramic potentiometers) linked to the mixer's left and right channels. They increase the level fed to one side at the expense of the other.

Stereo sources e.g. turntables, tape machines, are linked to two channel faders whose controls are ganged so that left and right levels are controlled simultaneously. A switch may also be incorporated to change stereo output to mono.

Pre-fade key and pre-set gain
A pre-fade (pre-hear or audition) key switch allows sources to be monitored without being faded up in the programme by switching them to a separate line to which meters, loudspeakers and headphones may be connected. A pre-set or coarse gain control is fitted to each module so that level can be set on pre-fade. Once set, this is the maximum level attainable when the fader is fully open.

Other controls
Fader modules vary in their degree of sophistication: some have built in controls for echo, public address, monitoring level, and frequency response. Frequency controls range from simple units for adjusting bass and treble to more complicated devices for controlling specific frequency ranges.

Microswitches are fitted to faders so that equipment can be remotely controlled from the mixer. They are also used for activating relays for cutting studio loudspeakers and switching on red warning lights whenever microphone faders are opened.

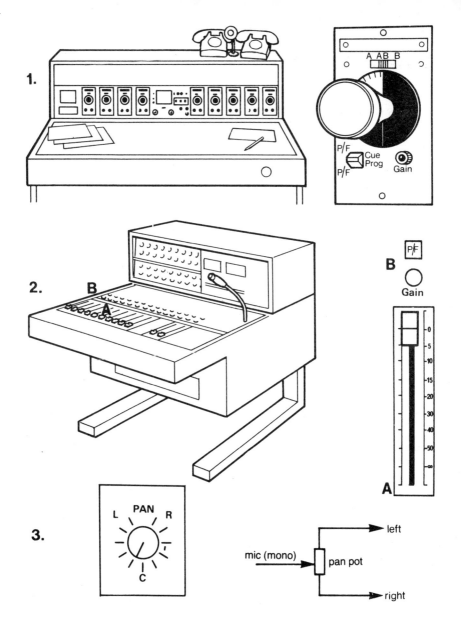

FADER MODULES

1. Large rotating faders are still used in some studios. Black semi-circular plates attached to the knobs show how far the channel has been faded up. 2. Modern mixer modules use slider faders A, pre-fade and coarse gain controls; B, may be built into the module or placed on an adjacent panel. This also applies to frequency correction controls, C. 3. Pan pots may be used to give a mono source a stereo image.

Taking Level

Sources should always be listened to as well as checked on a meter (and the levels adjusted, if necessary) before mixing.

Controls

A pre-fade (pre-hear or audition) key switch associated with the appropriate fader on the mixer allows the source to be monitored on a loudspeaker (or headphones) and meter without being faded up on air. Meters are either exclusively assigned to the pre-fade chain (audition buss) or have to be switched to it. A pre-set control on the fader is turned to reduce or increase the signal to the correct level.

Tapes and discs

On tape inserts and discs with short periods of excessive level, the pre-set is adjusted to suit the low levels and the fader set back to accommodate the high passages during the programme. This can be rehearsed if there is time. Pop music and talks stations in some countries take only a rough level check when they are regularly using only a small group of sources and let limiters and compressors reduce volume automatically, though at stations with a mixed format, where mixers are used for a variety of purposes, the level is checked either by the presenter or an operator. Classical music should never be compressed automatically so when playing discs it is essential to check level and allow for adjustment, if necessary.

Microphone level

Voice strength varies from person to person and their distance from the microphone. It often takes time to obtain a good balance with a guest and plenty of speech is needed for positioning the microphone and adjusting the pre-set. A favourite question to keep them talking is to ask what they had for breakfast. Contributors in remote studios will also talk endlessly about the weather if asked to do so!

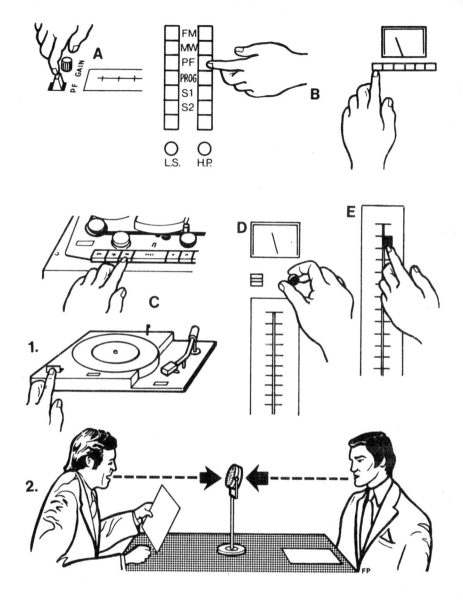

TAKING LEVEL

1. Equipment: A, the pre-fade switch of the appropriate fader is pressed; B, headphones (or loudspeakers) and meter may also have to be switched to the pre-fade chain; C, to obtain level on disc and tape, machines have to be started locally; D, the coarse gain or pre-set potentiometer is adjusted to give correct levels on the meter; E, fine adjustments may be made on the fader when on-air. 2. Taking level on voices. The microphone is placed to pick up an adequate sound signal and discriminate against noise and room colouration. Balancing is essential when more than one speaker share the same microphone. Pre-fade level and microphone placing are adjusted to suit all the speakers without much extra on-air control.

Manual Control

The volume of individual sources or programmes can be controlled manually on mixer faders or by automatic methods. The process of fading sources in and out is carried out manually during a programme.

Balance

The term 'balance' can be applied to individual microphones and when mixing two or more sources. A speaker or musical instrument is balanced by setting at a suitable distance away from the microphone and at the right level on the mixer.

Individual microphone levels are balanced on faders, when recording music for example, to achieve the correct blend of instruments. Discussions are treated in a similar way so that one speaker does not seem much louder than another. When speakers raise their voices the level has to be adjusted accordingly. Necessary control of music and speech has to be anticipated so that levels can be gently smoothed out. The fader is adjusted gradually so that high peaks and low level sound, normally outside the limits, remain within the dynamic range of the system. Sudden movements of the fader become noticeable, especially when they do not correspond to the dips or peaks encountered.

Music is controlled over a wider range than speech and needs gentler adjustment. The delicate balance of classical music is destroyed by automatic compressors so is always balanced manually in gradual steps.

Mixing

A complete programme is put together using a mixer through which various sources are routed, the levels of each being adjusted to fit within the dynamic range of the system and suit domestic listening conditions, so that music, studio speech, telephone inserts etc., are all smoothly balanced without disturbing differences in volume.

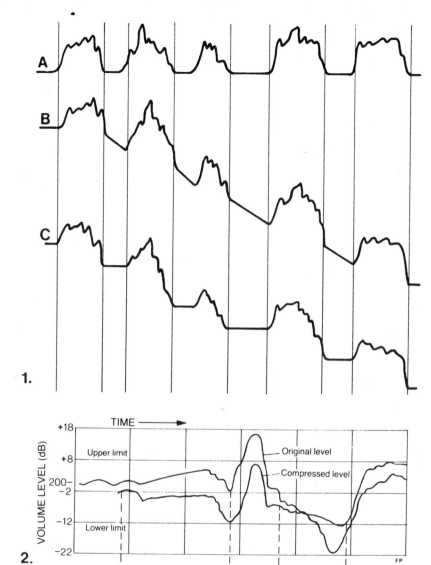

1.

2.

MANUAL CONTROL

1. **Controlling speech**

A, Sound varies continuously and consists of an interrupted series of peaks and troughs; B, manual compression should occur during gaps or, rapid fluctuations, thus keeping much of the original shape; C, a fade out is carried out smoothly and continuously when an obvious fade for dramatic effect e.g. a change of scene, is required.

2. **Manual control of programme volume**

The signal is compressed to fall between upper and lower limits, yet retain the same dramatic effect.

Levels

The difference between low and loud passages in music and speech, as well as between different programmes, is reduced in radio to provide a more even sound level.

It would be undesirable under normal listening conditions to recreate the same degree of loudness as in a concert hall for example, because most listeners would simply turn down their volume controls. Any speech that followed would be relatively inaudible, so requiring the listener's volume control to be increased. The radio station therefore smooths out these extreme differences to provide easier listening and also to fit within the dynamic range of the broadcasting system.

Dynamic range

The dynamic range is the difference between the lowest and highest permissible levels. Loud levels which would cause distortion along the transmission chain have to be reduced and those at low level increased to raise them above the noise present, whilst maintaining a relative difference when listened to. Stations concerned solely with speech are able to peak consistently higher levels on the meter than those used in a mixed format, because of the reduced need to maintain relative levels between items.

Matching of levels between items is very important on mixed format stations. It can also affect the style of all music stations. Live music and speech are controlled (balanced) to fit within the station's prescribed levels, sometimes using automatic control (see p. 30). When broadcasting recorded items less control over levels is needed. Once the tape or disc has been lined up after taking level, it should keep within the dynamic range, though classical music on disc may need manual adjustments because record reproducing equipment is capable of a wider dynamic range than that used in broadcasting. Pop music on disc is usually so heavily compressed it requires no further control, in fact PPM needles hardly move on some records. Automatic compression is never used in classical music programmes.

Range of levels

Generally, the range of levels attainable in speech is much less than in music. Telephone inserts are often peaked higher than normal speech to improve clarity. Although the meter on the control desk is a guide, the ear is the best judge for maintaining relative levels.

In serious music, the operator mixing the programme follows a musical score to anticipate low and loud passages so that manual adjustments can be made to keep the music within the dynamic range of the broadcasting system.

Programme Levels

Levels on a mono PPM for a station with mixed output. All music and all speech stations have a narrower range of levels.

Programme type	Normal peak	Range min	max
Commercials	4	2	4
News and weather	4½	4	6
Talks, drama, documentaries, panel games and quiz shows	5	3	6
Telephone inserts	5½	4	6
Light music, brass, dance and variety	–	2	6
Serious music	–	1*	6
Pop records, containing high degree of compression	4	2	4
Record programmes and live pop shows not containing high degree of compression	5	2	6
Announcements between music, depending on type of music	5	4	5
Applause	3	2	5
GTS	4	–	–

* or lower, without warning to engineering staff, for up to half a minute

Automatic Control

Automatic compressors contain amplifiers and work by reducing the gain (amplification) of a signal beyond a set level—the threshold point. Reduction of gain does not occur until the input level passes beyond that set point. Level below is unaffected but level above is automatically reduced by decreasing the amplifier gain for a moment. The degree of gain reduction, which is adjustable, is called the compression ratio i.e. the proportion of the additional volume reduced. The time taken for the system to restore to normal gain after a high level has passed is the recovery time. In a similar way, the time taken before the compressor acts following a sudden increase is the attack time. These three are also adjustable on many compressors. By increasing the compressor input level the low levels are increased, whilst the unit holds back the high levels, thus keeping the programme within a set range of levels.   Compression is used to a great extent in pop music and may also be used to sort out any errors in level. Compressors may also be used to reduce the level of one source whenever another is received. This is a form of automatic mixing and used in pop music programmes for voicing over the music.

When a microphone signal is fed into a voice over unit it automatically causes attenuation of the music signal. Sometimes a fair degree of control is possible as on ordinary limiters: fade down time, timing, degree of attenuation, and fade up time.

Transmission

Recorded programmes which are already compressed should not be compressed further on transmission, though all programme output is limited to protect transmitter circuits from being overloaded. VHF (FM) transmitters are equipped with limiters to prevent the programme being overmodulated into adjacent channels and distorting.

Limiters are a form of compressor. When a high compression ratio is used the output signal does not rise much above the threshold level, and so acts as a limiter. The signal is also compressed for medium wave transmissions to improve the signal to noise ratio. Compressors and limiters for stereo broadcasting have linked gain controls to prevent the stereo image shifting.

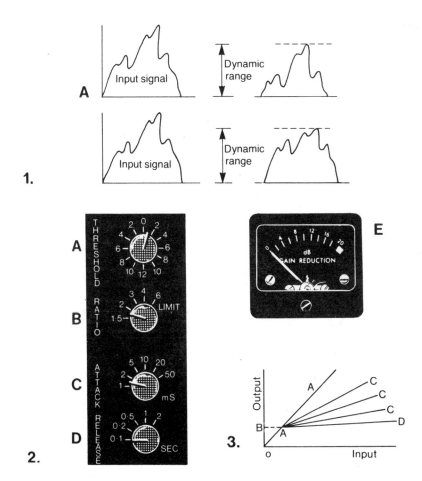

AUTOMATIC CONTROL

1. Control. A, Manual control keeps the sound within the dynamic range and retains the same 'shape'; B, limiters reduce the gain automatically to contain the peaks. 2. Compressor controls. A, Threshold level—the point at which compression begins; B, ratio—the degree of gain reduction; C, attack time—time before compressor acts; D, release (or delay) time—time before compressor releases its action; E, attenuation meter. 3. Settings. A, Linear operation with corresponding input and output levels, i.e. zero setting; B, adjustable threshold level for onset point of compression; C, various compression ratios available; D, heavy compression limits the maximum output volume close to the threshold level.

31

Meters

Levels can be checked accurately on a meter lined up using a standard reference tone. Relative sound intensities are measured in decibels (dB).

The meters on control boards are used for checking pre-fade (audition) levels, and board and station outputs. Two or three meters are often mounted on each board. For stereo work the A and B channels are either monitored on separate meters with a third for the mono output, or on special stereo units.

One or two of the board meters are usually linked to a multiway or rotary switch or pre-fade chain (audition buss) so that a variety of sources or outputs can be checked as required.

Peak Programme Meter (PPM)

Broadcasting studios in the UK use PPMs. These meters measure signal level and indicate peaks of programme. A special amplifier is used to achieve a regular scale over almost the whole working range. The graduations roughly correspond to equal changes in loudness. 6 represents 100% modulation with increases of 4 dB between divisions from 2 to 6. The difference between 0 and 1, and 1 and 2 is not so clearly defined on some meters but is often taken to be 4 dB although the area on this part of the meter is not as great as the other divisions. The white pointer is easy to read against a black background and has a fast rise time to register peaks, and a slow decay time which helps to reduce eye strain. Line-up or test tone should read 4.

Stereo PPMs have two needles in different colours to differentiate between left and right. Although more expensive than single movement meters they are easier to read than two separate meters.

VU meters

VU meters are marked in percentage modulation with an irregular decibel scale −20 to +3. More than half the scale is taken up by a range of 6 dB above and below 100% modulation. Most sound varies over a much greater area, so the needle moves more erratically than on a PPM. VU meters are cheaper than PPMs because of their simpler construction.

Bar graph meters

These are in widespread use in Europe and Scandinavia. A strip of a hundred or so glowing elements (light emitting diodes – leds) indicate level which appears as a pencil of light lengthening (or shortening) in sympathy with programme modulation. The electronics and scale of a bar graph meter can be made to suit any characteristic e.g. PPM or VU. They are also available in double strips for stereo work.

METERS

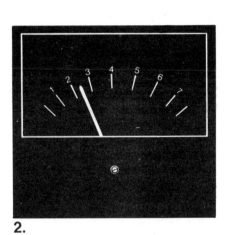

1.

1. Volume Unit (VU) meter (which can be illuminated).

2.

2. Peak Programme Meter (PPM).

3. Stereo PPM, coloured needles are used.

3.

Frequency Correction

Different parts of the frequency response can be increased or decreased in level by using an equalizer. Modules are either incorporated with individual faders, or as separate units which can be plugged to channels as required. They are also known as response selection amplifiers. The simplest type has controls for adjusting bass and treble whereas more elaborate modules allow particular bands to be reduced or increased. Narrow bands of middle frequencies (presence) may be boosted by different degrees to improve clarity.

Top cut and loss of top
Surface noise on old shellac 78 rpm records can be reduced by filtering out the high frequencies (top cut or roll off). Some turntable units are equipped with switches for top cut whereas on others an ordinary equalizer is used. Tape recordings with a poor signal to noise ratio caused by low recording levels can be improved slightly by removing some of the tape hiss. Occasionally top, high-frequency level is boosted, particularly in radio car transmissions to ensure a better signal back to base where the top can then be reduced. Loss of high frequencies causes a loss of clarity, equalizers help to smooth out the frequency response unless certain frequencies are extinct to begin with. The level of the lower frequencies can also be reduced or increased e.g. reducing the amount of bass when voices have been recorded too near to a ribbon microphone.

Midlift
Tapes recorded in noisy conditions may be improved by lifting or increasing a section of the middle frequencies, midrange boost. In music this can have the effect of picking out vocalists or particular instruments, and generally is used to improve clarity or separation.

Response shaping
The actual shape of a frequency response can be more accurately controlled using graphic equalizers which can boost or attenuate bands of frequencies. The shape can be set by moving sliders up or down for each band.

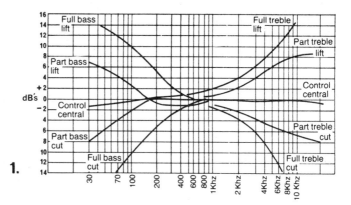

1.

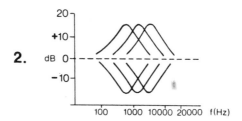

2.

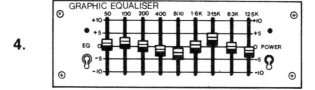

3.

4.

FREQUENCY CORRECTION

1. Equalizers are often fitted to individual mixer channels. They may be plugged up to channels when not fitted as standard equipment. Common controls include bass and treble lift and cut which work by adjusting the curve around a middle frequency. 2. Presence controls allow selected narrow bands of middle frequencies to be boosted (midlift) or cut. 3. Filters can introduce rapid fall off at either end of the frequency response. A, Base cut reduce bass to remove hum etc.; B, Top cut give a rapid fall off at the top end. 4. Graphic octave equalizer. Each slider controls the response of a separate octave. The arrangement of slides gives an indication of the response curve.

Cue and Talkback

A cue is an instruction to stop or start a particular operation or announce-ment, and may be visual or verbal. Cue programme is a feed of the pro-gramme. Tape inserts are accompanied by scripts giving the introduction to the tape. The words leading in to the tape provide the operator with a cue for starting the tape; the last words leading out of the tape (which are marked on the script) provide the operator and presenter with out cues.

Cue lights
Speakers are cued either by hand signals or by the flash of a small green light. A flickering light means speed up whilst a glowing light means slow down, though each station has its own variations. One flash during a news programme might be arranged to mean 'drop further items of bulletin' or 'the next item is ready'. A cue light is associated with each studio mic-rophone and operated by pressing a key switch or button on the control board. In local radio cue lights cannot normally be extended to other studios, nor outside broadcasts. Incoming calls on studio telephones are indicated on lamps instead of bells (which are disconnected). Different coloured covers are used to indicate different lines.

Talkback
Instructions may be passed from studio to control room (or other studios) and vice versa on an intercom system. A key is pressed which routes either a separate talkback or studio microphone onto the talkback circuit. Talkback can be heard on a loudspeaker or headphones. Normally the talkback feed to the studio speaker is cut whenever a microphone fader is opened otherwise instructions would be heard on air.

On-air cues are passed over headphones linked to the same circuit. When the talkback key is in the normal position the programme is heard on loudspeaker and headphones and is replaced by talkback when the key is pressed. When studio microphones are used for talkback purposes the key in the studio often acts as a microphone cut button, by switching the microphone from mixer to talkback amplifier. Cue programme to outside broadcasts and remote studios is sent by control line (see p. 14) or over a VHF talkback frequency for radio car inserts. During rehearsals, talkback can be left on the studio loudspeaker so that headphones do not have to be used.

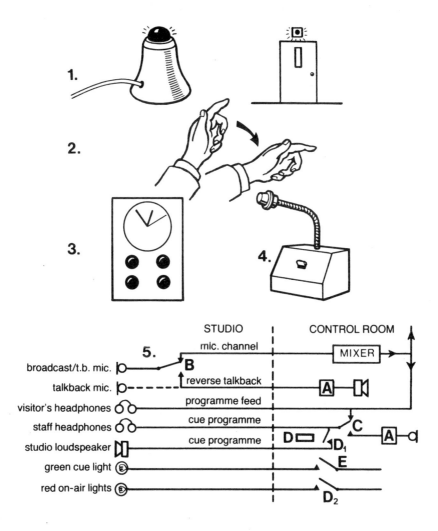

STUDIO   CONTROL ROOM

5.

mic. channel

MIXER

broadcast/t.b. mic. **B**

talkback mic.   reverse talkback   **A**

visitor's headphones   programme feed

staff headphones   cue programme

studio loudspeaker   cue programme   **D**   **C**   **A**

  D₁

green cue light   **E**

red on-air lights   **D₂**

CUE AND TALKBACK

1. Portable table top lamp units are used for signalling—red for on-air, green for cueing. Red lights are mounted above studio and control room doors. 2. Hand cues between operator and speaker, and two speakers. 3. Clock units often include lamp units for telephone signalling (in the studio) as well as red on-air lights. 4. Talkback units may be mounted on mixer control panels or as separate boxes. Control boards use a separate microphone for talkback whereas talkback units on talks tables may use the studio microphone. 5. Simplified talkback and signalling system used when a separate control room is used with a studio.

A, Talkback unit consists of a microphone and loudspeaker connected to an amplifer and selector keys; B, studio switch for changing studio microphone into talkback microphone—also acting as a cut switch; sometimes a separate talkback microphone is used; C, control room talkback key; D, relay that cuts the studio loudspeaker (D1) whenever a microphone channel is opened and operates red on-air warning lights (D2); E, switch for green cue light.

Studio Tape Recorders

Studio-based programmes are recorded and played back on mains-operated machines built for daily and rigorous operation. Various professional models are available though local stations tend to choose only a few from the many available because they have come to rely upon them for ease of operation and maintenance. The basic operation is almost identical on all machines.

Mounting and controls

Tape recorders consist of a tape deck and amplifier unit, and are fitted either on free-standing wheels or mounted on a desk (or rack) and have input and output connectors for programme. Extra facilities such as meters, switches for remote or local operation, and sockets for headphones are added as required. Loudspeakers are not usually included in studio models.

Tape deck

Push buttons control the basic operations i.e. play (left to right), stop, wind forward, rewind, and record. Other switches and buttons are for changing tape speed (the standard local radio speed being 7½ ips), holding the tape against the heads, pausing, rewind speed, and timing, although not all these facilities are fitted to every machine. 10½ inch metal take-up reels accept programmes of just over one hour's duration at 7½ ips. Large hubbed reels are used to reduce tape tension though some machines have switches to adjust the tension when cine reels are used.

Heads

There are three heads on each machine, erase, record, and playback, each one being either full- or stereo half-track. During recording, tape is erased by the first head before passing over the second head for recording. Recordings are played back on the third head so it is possible to monitor a programme a fraction of a second after it has been recorded.

Cleaning

Dirt or wax from editing pencils considerably reduces head efficiency so parts of the tape transport system i.e. heads, guides and capstan (but not plastic or rubber parts) are kept clean by wiping regularly with head cleaning fluid or methylated spirits.

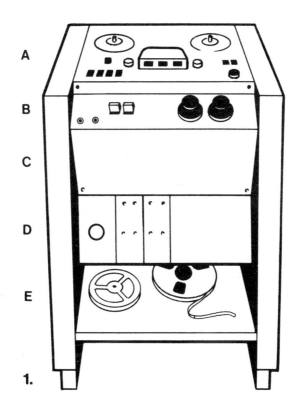

A

B

C

D

E

1.

2.

A   B   C   D   A   E   F

STUDIO TAPE RECORDERS

1. Trolley mounted tape recorders consist of A, tape deck with controls for stopping, starting, recording and spooling; B, monitoring and output controls—sockets for headphones, switches for local and remote control and faders for machine output; C, most decks and control apparatus have hinged panels for ease of maintenance; D, electronic apparatus—pre-amplifiers, recording and playback circuits, speed controls etc; E, stowage space. 2. Head assembly. A, Tape guides for keeping the tape aligned with the heads; B, erase head; C, record head; D, playback head; E, capstan spindle; F, pressure roller or pinch wheel.

Reels and Threading

Most inserts recorded on portable recorders are on plastic cine reels of 5 in diameter with a small hub, whilst the one for take-up on the right-hand side of a studio machine is likely to be a NAB 10½ in diameter metal reel with a large hub. Using the two kinds of reel on one machine creates excessive tension which causes slow starts and even tape damage especially when there is little tape on the smaller reel. Short inserts should be transferred to reels with larger hubs. Small plastic reels with large hubs are available for this purpose and will take about 10 minutes worth of material at 7½ ips. An alternative is to use a NAB metal reel to match that used for take-up but these obviously occupy far more room and make it difficult to handle lots of short items. Professional machines will take either, and adaptors are available for quickly converting from one to the other. Reels should be locked or screwed down to prevent them from lifting when rewinding.

Threading
The tape is threaded around the guides and spindles to smooth out tension variations and unevenly wound tape. The tape's emulsion side is on the inside of the reel and is the side which should face the tape heads. If the backing side is played there is a considerable drop in level especially of the high frequencies, and occurs when there is a twist in the tape, either on the spool or in the threading. The take-up reel needs a good grip of the tape so it is wise to test it first before rewinding otherwise it could stretch or snap the tape. Coloured leader tapes mark the beginning and end of tapes and is also used for threading up.

Items should begin where the tape joins the leader. The starting point should be set back to the left of the playback head. This allows time for the tape to reach full speed before passing the head. The actual distance will vary according to whether it is music or speech that is being played and the machine, but a safe way is to set the beginning over the erase head.

Starting
Tapes can be stopped and started by remote control, either by a switch on the control board for recording purposes or by opening the mixer fader. The controls for remote switching are often located on the front panel of the tape machine (see above).

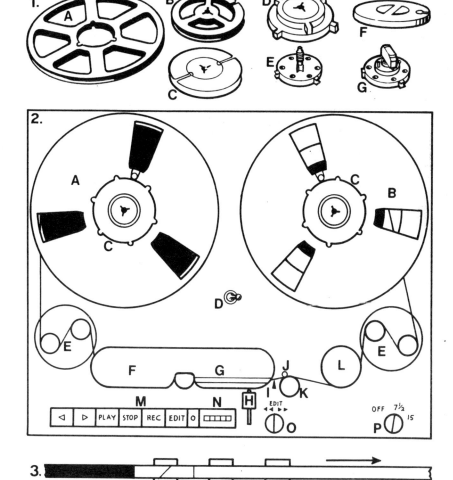

REELS AND THREADING

1. Reels and adaptors

A, 10½ in NAB metal reel with large hub; B, cine reel; C, 5 in plastic reel with large hub; D, NAB adaptor; F, DIN reel as used in parts of Europe; G, DIN adaptor.

2. Tape deck

A, Reel of tape (supply reel); B, NAB metal take-up reel; C, NAB adaptor; D, mono/stereo switch; E, capstans for electronic tape tension control; F, block containing erase, record and playback heads; G, tape splicing channel on top of head block; H, ink marker; I, mechanical scissors; J, drive capstan; K, pinch wheel; L, capstan for electronic speed control and timing; M, function buttons; N, timer in minutes and seconds; O, variable reeling speed control; P, speed selector for replay and record modes.

3. Replay position of tape

All inserts and programmes which have leaders fitted are lined up so the splice between tape and leader is over either the erase head or (for quicker starts on speech) on the record head, depending on how fast the machine runs up to full speed.

Tape Inserts

Several tape inserts may be used in a fast moving programme and in order to avoid confusion each reel is labelled with a short caption corresponding to the one at the top of the cue sheet e.g. 'Fire', 'Docks' etc. The duration is marked on the reel and on the script so that an accurate check can be kept during a programme. The cue sheet lists in and out cues on the tape (the first and last few words). When taking level on pre-fade (audition) the insert must be listened to as well as checked on the meter. This acts as a double check on in cues. Tape inserts are started by remote control by opening the mixer fader.

Leader on reels

Yellow or white leader is used at the beginning of mono recordings and red at the end. Other colours can be used to identify stereo tapes, speed etc., according to station policy. Enough leader should be attached to allow for threading and a couple of turns of the take-up reel. Leader is not used for cartridge inserts (see p. 44).

Bands

Inserts are best kept on separate spools or cartridges but where it is necessary to have two or more on one reel, yellow leader is inserted between items. This provides a silent point for stopping the tape and cueing it for the next item. Seven inches of tape are enough to do this in most cases. It is difficult to see shorter pieces in a reel and it does not give the operator enough time to close the fader. Longer pieces take time to wind on to the next cut. A time-saving way of resetting is to leave the fader slightly open (with the machine on remote control) at the end of the insert.

This allows the tape to continue moving but reduces the chance of hearing anything if it runs onto the next item. As the next insert comes up to the starting point the fader is closed which automatically stops the tape. The tape is then reset against the heads. The levels of the various bands should be checked beforehand and marked on the script. When rewinding tapes all faders for the channel must be closed even during editing because high-speed rewinding can cause cross talk on other lines. There is also the danger that if a mixer tape fader is accidentally left open the rewinding will be broadcast. The high speed chatter created when winding with the tape against the heads is also so powerful it can damage the loudspeakers.

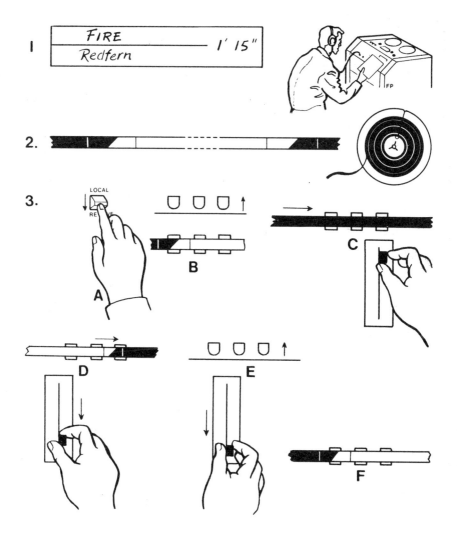

TAPE INSERTS

1. All tape inserts and recorded programmes should carry basic details. Introductions are listened to and checked with the cue sheet. 2. Several inserts may be banded together with short pieces of leader tape joining them. Bands of leader are seen as rings when several tape inserts are assembled on one reel. 3. The tape is checked for level and in cues, the tape machine (A) is switched to remote operation and the tape held against the heads (mechanically, B). The splice is then aligned against the erase head or other standard position used by the station. When the fader is opened (C) the tape starts and gathers full speed before passing the replay head. When inserts are multi-banded, time may be saved by keeping leaders running through with the fader slightly open (D). As the next band comes up the tape is stopped by closing the fader (E) and the tape depressed against the heads again and re-aligned (F) ready for replaying.

Cartridges

These should not be confused with cassettes which use narrower tape and can be wound in either direction.

Cartridges use ¼ in wide tape in an endless loop wound round a central drum. The tape passes from the centre of the core to a slot along one edge (similar to cassettes) and then through plastic guides to wind round the outside of the drum. Lubricated tape is used to provide smoother tape transport, and runs in one direction only. At the end of a recording the cartridge machine runs the tape on through the loop until the beginning has been reached again. This is marked by a burst of tone on a cue track and is automatically inserted on the tape whenever a recording is made (see p. 56).

Size
Various cartridge sizes are available with loop durations from a few seconds to 30 minutes. The longer the gap of blank tape at the end of a recording though, the longer it takes to recycle although some machines are able to rewind quickly. In broadcasting, the main use of cartridges is for short items including news reports and interviews, jingles, trailers, commercials and tags. Single and multiple machines are available for playback only, as well as more expensive versions for recording. Multicartridge machines are very useful when a station relies heavily on cartridge material. Larger machines hold cartridges vertically or around a drum and can be linked to automated broadcasted systems (see p. 56).

Recording
Items to be transferred to cartridge are assembled in complete form on an ordinary reel of tape. If the tape is being dubbed through a mixer, level is taken and the fader opened. The tape is then set on pause—ready to roll and with the beginning of the tape insert set well back to the left of the heads or even partly wound on the reel. The tape machine is then set in motion and as the beginning comes up to the playback head the cartridge machine is switched to record. Starting the playback machine first allows the cartridge to be recorded at precisely the right moment. When recording items direct from a network line or from a live voice piece without first using a reel-to-reel machine, it helps if a verbal countdown is given e.g. 'Going in 3, 2, 1' and then start the cartridge.

The cartridge machine continues until the starting point has been reached, and then stops. Alternatively, several separate items may be recorded on one cartridge. To do this, the cartridge is stopped at the end of each item and reset for the next recording. Recordings are always made on bulk-erased cartridges with the splice in the loop well past the heads. Splice and tape fault locaters are available to do this job automatically.

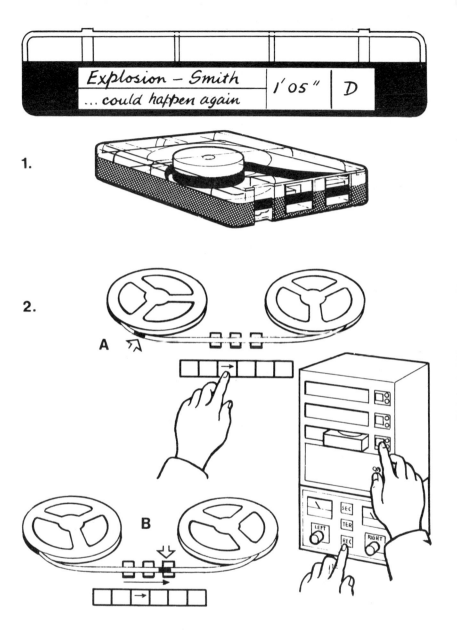

CARTRIDGES

1. Cartridges contain endless loops of tape wound onto a drum. Tape is drawn off from the centre of the core and rewound on the outside. Cartridges are labelled with a brief title, out cue, duration and reference. 2. Transferring from reel to cartridge. The tape is set in motion with the introduction well to the left of the heads. As the beginning comes up to the replay head the cartridge machine is switched to record.

Programme Monitoring

Levels are checked on meters (see p. 32) and programmes continuously monitored on high-quality loudspeakers (though a self-operating performer would listen to his output on headphones most of the time).

Loudspeakers and headphones
Stereo programmes are monitored on two loudspeaker units mounted each side of the control board. The sum of the A and B channels for mono service is also checked either on a speaker in another room or by switching the sum signal to one speaker only. There should not be any obstruction between the loudspeakers and operator.

Loudspeaker volume is a matter of personal judgement but most operators prefer to listen at fairly high level compared with domestic conditions. The lower domestic listening level must be taken into account though when monitoring because high listening levels can give a completely false impression of what the programme sounds like to the listener. The studio loudspeaker is cut whenever microphone channels are opened so performers who self-operate their programmes wear headphones for monitoring the programme output. Any technical or operational faults are then noticed. Headphones are also worn when there is a separate operator for receiving on-air instructions and pre-fading (auditioning) sources. When programmes are operated from a separate control room the headphones are switched to a feed of control room talkback and cue. During a recording the operator should also check the tape on playback (see p. 134).

Ring main
Meters, loudspeakers and headphones may be switched to a variety of facilities, including the pre-fade chain for lining up and monitoring sources on the mixer channels, and a selection of outputs. In some cases these are grouped together on a multiway switch called a ring main or rotary switch including outputs from the studio, transmitter, networks etc. When the preceding programme is coming from another studio the station output is listened to for the station break. Once the programme is underway, the studio output can be monitored direct unless no one is available to monitor transmitter output. Performers should never stop broadcasting even if programme disappears from the headphones until confirmation is received from engineering staff. If programme is being monitored on the VHF transmission and it disappears it does not necessarily mean that other feeds are faulty; many stations have several outputs: VHF, medium wave and relay services.

ROTs
Recordings of station output or that of other transmissions are called ROTs (recording-off-transmission) off-line or airchecks. They are used for repeats of live programmes, obtaining material from other networks and reference purposes.

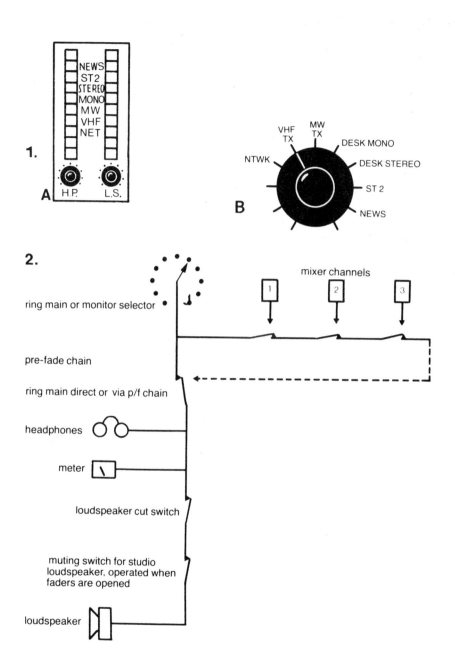

1.

A H.P. L.S.

NEWS
ST 2
STEREO
MONO
MW
VHF
NET

B

VHF TX
MW TX
DESK MONO
DESK STEREO
ST 2
NEWS
NTWK

2.

ring main or monitor selector

mixer channels

1 2 3

pre-fade chain

ring main direct or via p/f chain

headphones

meter

loudspeaker cut switch

muting switch for studio
loudspeaker, operated when
faders are opened

loudspeaker

PROGRAMME MONITORING
1. Monitoring outputs. Headphones, loudspeakers and meters may be
switched to a variety of outputs for monitoring purposes either on a row of
buttons (A) or rotary switch (B). 2. Simplified monitoring system for control
room or self-operational studio control boards.

Stereo Transmission

Stereo programmes consist of two channels represented by the letters A and B for left and right respectively.

Pilot-tone system

There are several methods of transmitting stereo programmes but in the UK, Canada, USA and Japan, the pilot-tone system is used (also known as the Zenith GE or stereo multiplex system). The programme is encoded into two signals which are fed to the same VHF/FM transmitter. One signal is the sum of A and B (A + B). The other is the difference between the two channels (A − B or B − A, whichever is the greater). The transmitter inserts a fixed tone for reference whenever broadcasting in stereo. Domestic receivers use this tone for automatic switching from mono to stereo. Mono–stereo switching at the transmitter is performed by remote control from the studio. An inaudible tone is inserted in the programme leaving the station which triggers switching equipment at the transmitter.

Decoding

Mono receivers select only the A + B signal whilst stereo receivers are able to reproduce the separate A and B channels by processing (decoding) the two signals. This system has the advantage that mono receivers receive a mixture of the two channels thus creating a true monophonic performance rather than reproducing either A or B separately (which would need separate transmitters for A and B channels, and, of course, require the listener to use separate receivers).

Mono programmes

The transmitter may be switched to stereo or mono according to programme requirements. When a long mono programme is being broadcast the station usually switches the transmitter to mono so that listeners with automatic stereo decoders can obtain better signal quality. Instructions to the transmitter are sent over the programme lines by inserting short bursts of high frequency tone in a similar way to the automatic monitoring system (see p. 50).

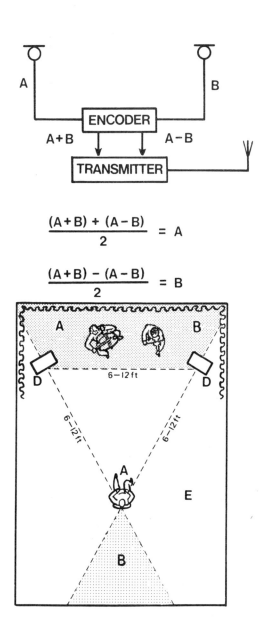

$$\frac{(A+B) + (A-B)}{2} = A$$

$$\frac{(A+B) - (A-B)}{2} = B$$

STEREO TRANSMISSION
1. Stereo receivers record the information by an addition and subtraction process. Mono receivers use only the sum signal. 2. Recommended listening position in living room or studio. A, Ideal position; B, area giving good listening; C, area where sound seems to be produced; D, loudspeakers, away from the wall; E, carpeted floor and soft furnishings, including heavy curtains.

Transmitter Monitoring

Transmitters are usually sited some distance away from the studio because of the limited space available in city centres and also to take advantage of higher areas away from building obstructions.

Lines
Two music lines are used to link the station with the VHF transmitter. Stations broadcasting in mono use one line to broadcast on and keep the second as a reserve. At stations capable of broadcasting in stereo a matched pair of lines is used between studio and transmitter. If a fault occurs in one line the station reverts to a mono service and combines the left- and right-hand signals onto the other line. Only one music line is normally used to serve local radio medium wave transmitters.

Monitoring
Most local radio transmitters are unmanned and as transmitter faults are not always obvious they could go unnoticed until a break in transmission occurs, so automatic monitoring systems are incorporated at the transmitters to assess any maintenance required. Information from the monitor can be sent in coded form over an ordinary telephone line, in which case a series of pips or buzzes are heard in a set order to check the items functioning normally and those which are faulty.

Another method involves coded electronic messages at an inaudible high frequency inserted in the transmissions. These signals are detected by monitoring equipment at the studio which triggers lights for particular faults, on a display panel. The equipment shows the operator the basic type of fault. Most automatic monitors show any changeover to reserve transmitter, line loss, loss of programme and even mast or tower light failure. In a similar way, the stereo transmitter can be remotely switched to mono or stereo by pressing a button on the studio control board. This inserts an inaudible signal in the programme sent to the transmitter, where equipment deciphers the signal and performs the switch over.

Reserve equipment
Several sections of many transmitters are duplicated so that if a fault occurs, reserve equipment can be switched into service. In case of line failure, some medium wave transmitters are capable of switching over to a feed from a receiver tuned to the station's VHF service. In this way a spare line feed to medium wave local radio transmitters is unnecessary.

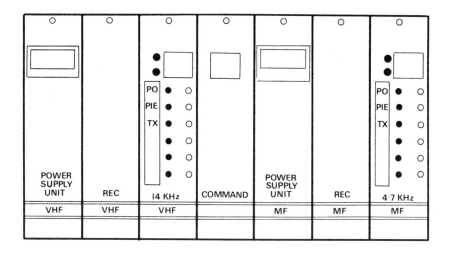

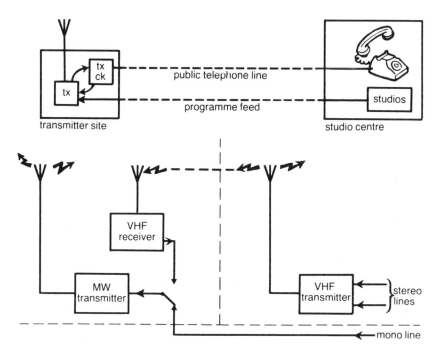

TRANSMITTER MONITORING
1. Over-air signalling unit. These modules are normally fitted in the apparatus room bays at the studio centre. Coloured lights indicate the condition of the transmitter and programme input equipment. This information is sent automatically in coded form over the air. 2. Interrogating by telephone. Transmitter checking equipment may be linked to public telephone lines. The check sequence is initiated by dialling the transmitter's telephone number. 3. Alternative source. If either of the stereo lines breaks down a mono service can be supplied on the remaining line.

Master Control Room (MCR)

Programmes may originate from many different sources but all have to be switched at some central point for feeding the transmitters. This is performed on a studio or control room mixer board. At stations with more than one studio, one is assigned to feed the transmitters and is known as the MCR. The other studios and sources are then routed through the MCR for transmission. As well as being a switching and monitoring point, the MCR is also used for programme production either as a self-operational board or in conjunction with a separate studio. Facilities include a mixer, jackfield (apparatus or rack bay), transmitter switching and monitoring equipment, tape and cartridge machines, turntables and microphones.

Two-board system

As described in an earlier section, there is very little difference between control rooms and studios. In actual practice it is usual for two studios to be fitted with control boards and equipped as self-operational studios which can also be used as control rooms with separate studios. Transmitter output may be switched from one board to another thus allowing absolute flexibility. At stations where transmitter control is regularly switched from one board to the other a keyswitch or pushbutton is mounted on the control panel for changing control. At others it may be mounted on the apparatus bay in either of the rooms. Very often one room is used as a self-operational studio feeding the other which is used as the MCR. In this case, the MCR takes the studio output as a source on one of the faders and mixes in other items including promotions etc., as required. Maintenance can also be easily carried out if one board has to be taken out of service since control and operations are transferred to the other desk.

Although two-board systems have separate mixers and reproducing and recording equipment in each room they do share certain common facilities. Outside sources and lines from the apparatus bay are duplicated so that feeds can be taken on either board. It is also possible with some systems to operate the other room's microphones e.g. a newsreader's microphone may be faded up by a DJ from the studio desk or by an operator in the MCR when one desk is feeding the other. They may also share a third studio which may be controlled from either mixer.

Direct to transmitter

Stations which take networked programmes for long periods can use both desks and associated equipment for other purposes, when not used for live transmission, by switching the network line direct to the transmitters instead of through the mixer. It is also possible to switch other sources, including tape recorders, direct to the transmitters.

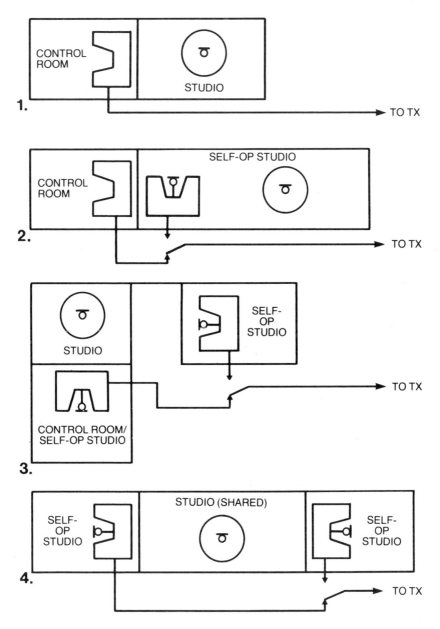

CONTROL ROOM

Examples of control switching arrangements

1, Simple routing of all programmes through one control room with its own studio; 2, similar to 1, but with control board in studio as well for self-operated programmes—sources being shared by the two boards, and output from one or other switched as required to the transmitter; 3, transmitter control from either self-operating studio or control room; 4, transmitter control from either of two self-operating studios sharing a common studio facility as well.

53

Taking Control

At stations where transmitter control is regularly switched from board to board, care has to be taken to avoid programmes being taken off the air unintentionally, or creating sudden jumps in level.

Simple change-overs
Where transmitter control is available on either of two boards, with one of them mixing a programme live (i.e. the board direct to the transmitter) and the other about to take the next programme, control can be taken in a short pause between programmes.

When one programme ends from the other studio and another programme begins without any overlap, it is possible to flick the control key or button just before starting the programme, but when a hand-over from one presenter to another is required with the outputs of the two studios heard simultaneously, a fader has to be used. The same situation occurs when the presenter of the following programme is using both hands to start equipment and needs control in advance.

Change-overs on a fader
To take control of a programme coming from another studio, a feed of the on-air studio is selected on the switchable fader of the mixer. Sometimes a fader is permanently allocated for this purpose and pre-set so that when fully opened it will give levels matching those leaving the on-air board. On other boards the programme is selected on a multiway switch or automatic switching matrix linked to a fader. In the case of multiway switches, the level has to be adjusted to match the station output level, by comparing levels on separate PPMs. Switching matrix systems often provide sources at their correct levels. When the two readings are identical i.e. the pre-fade level is the same as the programme level on the on-air board, and the programme fader is open, control can be taken.

Precautions
Before opening the programme fader prior to taking control, make absolutely certain that the on-air mixer is not taking a feed of the board otherwise a feedback will occur (with the two taking a feed of each other). Make sure also, that no other source is unintentionally faded up, and that the board is functioning normally (according to station instructions). When switching from one board to another make sure that they are in identical modes i.e. both taking the same network or are switched to mixer output.

Direct to transmitter
Some control boards have extra keys or buttons fitted to enable tape machines and lines e.g. network, to be switched direct to the transmitter, thus freeing the mixer and equipment for other uses (see p. 46).

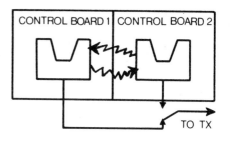

CONTROL BOARD 1 | CONTROL BOARD 2

TO TX

Feed back
A check is made to ensure the on-air desk is not taking a feed off the board.

Programme feed
A feed of the on-air board is selected on a mixer channel.

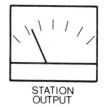

PRE-FADE

STATION OUTPUT

Comparison
The channel is monitored on pre-fade and levelled with that on the output meter.

PF   GAIN

TX CONTROL

1   2

Control
When the levels match, the fader may be fully opened and control taken.

Automated Broadcasting

Junctions involve a series of switching operations which may be performed automatically and include stopping and starting tapes, selecting and fading up sources, operating cue lights, and joining network.

Replaying programmes
Automatic switching systems can switch to live or recorded sequences, and work from programmed instructions and cues recorded on tapes and time clocks. Instructions are programmed to select recorded items and live sources in a set daily order. Programmes may be replayed, for transmission, on reel-to-reel machines. Very often several programmes are compiled onto one reel. Simple switching systems change over from machine to machine at the ends of programmes, and may be controlled by a time clock or small switching unit.

More advanced systems use switching units which can perform the whole range of operations normally associated with manual operations at station breaks. Short items are replayed in the usual way from cartridges; several cartridges may be held in a drum without an operator to insert them.

Switching
Short bursts of tone are recorded onto the ends of each programme for triggering the next switching sequence. Programmes on reel-to-reel machines have bursts of 25 Hz tone recorded on the actual programme track. This is filtered out and does not affect normal transmission. When the tone is sensed, the switching unit fades down one source and cues (if live) or starts and fades up the next source. When the tone stops the switch stops the machine and it is then ready for the next programme recorded on that reel.

Cartridge machines employ a slightly different system. Switching cues are recorded on separate cue tracks, and use different tones for different purposes. All cartridges whether played manually or triggered automatically have a primary cue tone recorded at the beginning of the recording. When replaying cartridges, the machine continues running until the beginning of the tape loop has been reached. When the tape has been fully recycled the burst of primary tone is sensed by the machine and the tape is stopped. A secondary burst of tone of 150 Hz may be recorded on the cue track at the end of the recording. A tertiary tone of 8 Hz may be recorded for operating ancillary equipment whilst automatic logging systems may use another tone for describing the item to be logged.

Ancillary equipment
Details of automatic operations including transmission times and technical faults can be printed out automatically. Cartridge systems using secondary and tertiary tone switching may be linked up.

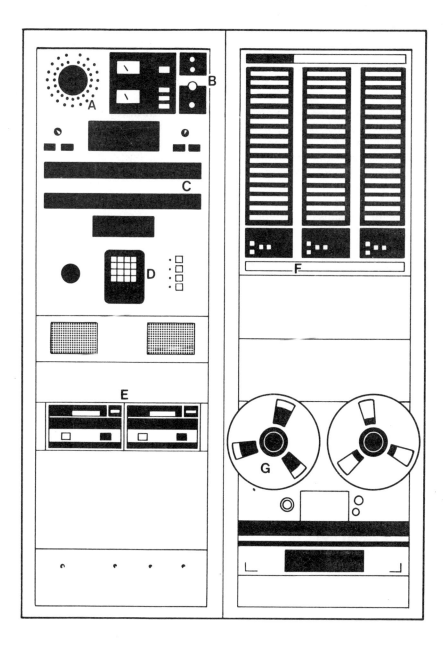

AUTOMATED BROADCASTING

A, Control unit showing which source is on-air and next event; B, monitoring meters and switches together with start/stop manual controls; C, switch type memory giving sequence of events; D, keys for programming the unit; E, two single cartridge machines for commonly used items e.g. station idents; F, multiple cartridge machine for commercials (though they can be used for programmes); G, reel-to-reel tape machine replaying programmes.

Details of output are kept in a log.

Logging

Worldwide, most radio stations are required by law or regulations to keep a record of items broadcast including content, duration, junctions (or breaks), with details of commercials and promotions. Methods of logging vary but fall into four basic categories: technical; programme; music; and commercial; though some may be combined in a single log.

Technical log
This is for transmission or equipment faults, and operational errors, and may be used for noting regular transmitter checks.

Programme log
The programme or station log is the main record of station output. It includes basic details: transmission times, programme titles or items and often programme content, names of presenters, reporters, interviewees etc., and source of material. Details of individual programmes may be written up as part of a continuous log or kept separate. These are filed under Programmes as Broadcast (P as B).

Music log
Music is logged for payment of royalties and fees, and as a record of needletime, this is the total number of hours of commercially produced records a station may play each day. Commercial records do not normally count as needletime when played for the first time as part of a record review. Radio stations often have their records free from needletime restrictions specially produced for presentation, promotions, and commercials. Music logs vary in the amount of information required which may be selected from: title; name of lp or group; composer; arranger; record label; numbers; and on-air duration.

Commercial log
An accurate check is made of all commercials broadcast (or not broadcast) and includes time of transmission, name of commercial, and duration. It may be combined with the technical or programme log to give the name of the programme during which the commercial breaks occur and regular transmission checks.

Automated logging
Some automatic broadcasting systems (see p. 56) can be programmed to print out transmission details. Most stations also keep ROTs, these are usually made at low speed e.g. $1\frac{5}{16}$ ips, so several hours recording may be made without changing reels. Four track recorders are useful for logging.

A log of station output is kept by all stations.

JUNCTION	PROGRAMME /ITEM		DETAILS / SPEAKERS	DUR
12 15.00	Farming Today	Tape	(separate log.)	29'30"
1244.30	Prog. info.	live	next week	
			Gardener's Question Time	22"
	Ident + time			
	check + intro			8"
1245.00	Outlook		Presented by C. Letts	
	STRIKE	R.CAR	SWAIN	
	UNION	TAPE	BILL GREEN/SWAIN	
	BRIDGE	"	CLR. SMITH/LAING	
	NEWS	LIVE	RAWSON	
	HOUSING	TAPE	VOX POP RESIDENTS +	
			CLR MOORE/LAING	

Some organisations require that stations keep a recorded copy of all transmission for reference, usually at 15/16 ips.

1	LEFT STEREO PROG.
2	RIGHT " "
3	MONO PROG.
4	TIME SIGNAL (SPEAKING CLOCK)

Print out machines may be linked to some automated systems.

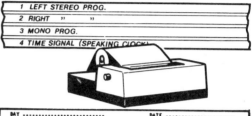

DAY ....   DATE ....

LOGGED BY:

.................ON.....OFF.....   ...............ON.....OFF.....
.................ON.....OFF.....   ...............ON.....OFF.....
.................ON.....OFF.....   ...............ON.....OFF.....

FOR NAMES OF LOCAL OR   NETWORK PROGRAMS SEE ATTACHED LOG..........

COMMERCIAL MATTER OR ANNOUNCEMENT TYPE   PROGRAM TYPE

CM---COMMERCIAL MATTER   A-----AGRICULTURAL
PSA--PUBLIC SERVICE ANNOUNCEMENT   E-----ENTERTAINMENT
NCA--NON-COMMERCIAL ANNOUNCEMENT   PA----PUBLIC AFFAIRS
MRA--MECHANICAL REPRODUCTION ANNOUNCEMENT R-----RELIGIOUS
                                     S-----SPORTS
PROGRAM SOURCE   I-----INSTRUCTIONAL
                                     O-----OTHER
STN ID--STATION IDENTIFICATION   EDIT--EDITORIAL
NET-----NBC NETWORK   POL---POLITICAL
V. T.---VOICE TRACK   ED----EDUCATIONAL
WX------WEATHER
ST NOW--STEP NOW
S. S.---SILENCE SENSE
C LOOP--CLOSED LOOP
XTR ON--TRANSMITTER ON
XTROFF--TRANSMITTER OFF

TIME   SOURCE   PROGRAM/COMMERCIAL MATERIAL   LENGTH TYPE
---------- ------   ----------------------------------   ------ ----
11:56:24AM 14 00 MUSIC
11:58:47AM 15 00 FILL
11:59:55AM 05 00 STN ID
12:00:00P M 19 00 NET
12:03:31PM ******ST NOW
12:03:31PM 03 00 NEWS
12:05:03PM 06 00 JINGLE
12:05:07PM 11 00 MUSIC
12:08:23PM 16 00 V. T.
12:08:24PM 12 00 MUSIC
12:11:50PM 10 00 TIME
12:11:53PM 01 15 MCDONALDS (BREAKFAST)   :30 CM
12:12:23PM 01 44 SEARS/AUTOMOTIVE   :60 CM
12:13:24PM 01 01 DRUG ABUSE CENTER   :10 PSA
12:13:36PM 06 00 JINGLE
12:13:40PM 16 00 V. T.
12:13:41PM 13 00 MUSIC
12:15:02PM ******XTROFF
12:16:14PM*14*30*MUSIC
12:17:13PM*******XTR ON
12:19:33PM 04 00 WX
12:20:02PM 02 05 RECORD GALAXY/W. B. RECORDS   :60 CM
12:21:01PM 01 11 JACK IN THE BOX   :30 CM
12:21:30PM 10 00 TIME
12:21:32PM 06 00 V. T.
12:21:36PM 16 00 V. T.
12:24:17PM 11 00 MUSIC
12:24:17PM 08 00 TEMP
12:24:17PM*******C LOOP
12:24:17PM 12 00 MUSIC
12:28:56PM 18 00 STUDIO
12:30:30PM*******ST NOW
12:30:30PM 06 00 JINGLE
12:30:33PM*******S. S.
12:30:33PM 16 00 V. T.
12:30:34PM 11 00 MUSIC

Print outs give brief details of items and transmission times.

59

Recordings for Transmission

Recorded programmes have to fit within allocated time slots, around which the station fits continuity announcements, trailers, news, commercials (promotions), and identification jingles as required. Programmes which end on music e.g. a signature tune, are easily run to time by back-timing (pre-fading) (see p. 82) the music to the out time of the programme. Programmes are very rarely allowed to over-run unless circumstances permit, and then only by prior arrangement. Under-runs, if allowed, are noted so that material can be prepared to fill the gap, a programme is never started early if the preceding one finishes early.

The producer
Recordings are checked by the producer/presenter responsible for the programme content. All splices are checked and care taken to ensure that all unwanted material, such as double takes (repeats), has been cut out. Time checks are not given in recorded programmes and any material which would 'date' is also left out, otherwise an introductory announcement has to be made saying when the programme was first broadcast or recorded.

Programmes to be repeated leave out news of events which will have passed by the time the repeat goes out. Information may also need updating. Details which are likely to change between the first and repeat transmission are best omitted from the tape and left for a continuity announcer to read. In this way, tape duration and structure remains unchanged. The same applies to automated systems. Updates can be recorded onto cartridges and inserted automatically before the programme tape. Automatic stations add bursts of tone at the ends of programmes to trigger switching sequences.

Transmission day
The whole day's programmes are checked in advance for timing, date, and details. In automatic systems, the tapes are assembled in sequence and loaded into the system. At manual stations, the tapes are left in a programme rack until needed. Some recorded programmes have a short period of tone recorded at zero level at the beginning of the tape. This allows the programme to be transmitted at exactly the same levels it was recorded at. Tone is made to read 4 (0 in US) on PPMs (stereo sum and mono meters).

After the tape has been lined up with the tape against the heads, the machine is switched to remote (see p. 110). The operator or presenter/announcer can then close the microphone and start the tape machine in one smooth action from the mixer desk.

After transmission, the tape is rewound and placed in the correct slot in the rack if it is to be repeated or returned to its producer.

RECORDED PROGRAMME

No. SP/78/41

| TITLE | WHAT A GAME | (PROG. 4 of 5 - RUGBY LEAGUE) |

| TX DATE AND TIME | **1** | 30.7.78 | at | 17.00 | **2** | 4.8.78 | at | 19.00 |

SPECIAL INSTRUCTIONS
After Sunday tx. place in Friday's rack

(7½)/15   MONO/~~STEREO~~

DUTY ANNOUNCER

(station ident and time check).

Sporting history now as we continue our story about the world's many different football games. Today Barrie Redfern looks at Rugby League.

TAPE BEGINS	DURATION TO END OF

on whistle and crowd fx with words "What a game!..."

		SPEECH		PROG	
		MIN	SEC	MIN	SEC

TAPE ENDS "....In the next programme, the last in the series, Barrie Redfern visits Australia and Ireland to find how the two countries developed their own distinctive kinds of football." (music to end).

| 29 | 35 | 29 | 42 |

DUTY ANNOUNCER

And that final programme can be heard, here on XYZ, at the same time, 5 o'clock, next Sunday afternoon.

Today's programme can be heard again on Friday evening at 7 o'clock.

| RECORDED BY WALKER | SIGNATURE OF PRODUCER OR PERSON RESPONSIBLE FOR PROGRAMME | *B. Redfern* |

1.

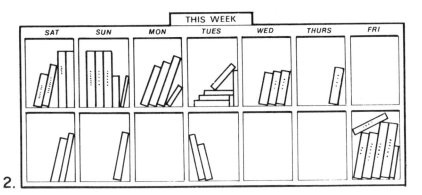

2.

RECORDINGS FOR TRANSMISSION

1. Cue sheet for recorded programmes at stations with a mixed format. 2. Stations which regularly broadcast recorded programmes often keep the tapes in a rack divided up into a space for each day.

Breaks and Junctions

Breaks are the intervals used on commercial stations during or after programmes for commercials, news, weather, and public service announcements (hence commercial break, newsbreak etc.).

Junctions are points at which programmes begin and end. In non-commercial broadcasting junctions between programmes are used only for continuity announcements.

Jingles
Station idents and other jingles are usually all that mark one programme ending and another beginning on commercial stations. Breaks are usually accompanied by jingles for leaving or joining programmes. Commercial breaks, for example, thus become easily identified as separate from programme material. Jingles are self-contained musical or music and speech packages and are not voiced over by presenters or overlayed by discs, though a few are designed to be segued with a second cartridge giving the presenter's name. Jingles are best given their full run unless they have a long fade out. In the same way, they should not be started over a disc or tape which has either not finished or not been faded out properly to fit the music. A full set of jingles is left in studio areas for commercial breaks, news, weather, programme introductions, and spots etc.

Commercials
In the UK these are pre-recorded onto cartridges. Various rules cover the playing of commercials and often require that: *a*, consecutive commercials do not use the same voice; *b*, a pause be left between two commercials ending and beginning on speech; *c*, commercials do not use the voice of the presenter or newsreader heard immediately before or after the break; and *d*, other material is not overlaid on commercials.

Continuity
Stations which have variable formats use live continuity announcements between programmes for linking, absorbing under-runs, and promoting programmes (see p. 64). A script is enclosed with each recorded programme for transmission and this tells the announcer or operator its duration, how it begins and ends, and gives introduction and back announcement details.

Junctions act as a buffer between different styles of programme e.g. in an extreme case between a Church service and a record request programme. The announcer smoothes the way from one programme to the next. He also expands or edits material to meet fixed times in the schedule e.g. joining network (see p. 148).

EXAMPLE OF NEWS AND COMMERCIAL BREAK, ALL PRESENTED LOCALLY.

DISC	(programme - faded or prefaded to time)
CARTRIDGE	(jingle - musical only)
NEWSREADER	This is Barrie Redfern with XYZ News at 9 o'clock. (news bulletin including tape and cartridge inserts)
	It's five past nine. Back in a moment with sports news from Charles Hall, and the weather.
CARTRIDGES	(commercial break)
CARTRIDGE	(end of commercial break musical sting)
SPORTSREADER	Now sport and .... (sports bulletin with tapes etc.)
NEWSREADER	Charles Hall. And the weather: .... (weather forecast) .... XYZ News at ten past nine.
CARTRIDGE	(jingle - D J 's name)
DISC	(programme - possibly with voice over music saying "Welcome back" etc.)

BREAKS AND JUNCTIONS

Good presentation is based on good planning and use of materials at junctions—written trails, recorded trails (on reel or cartridge), jingles and discs. A stop watch may be useful.

Promotions (Trailers)

Information about future programmes may be given out live or played from a tape. On mixed format stations, promotions tend to be used in junctions between programmes, whereas all-music and commercial stations usually include them within programmes.

The basic structure of all trailers consists of information about programme content and the time of transmission (day, date, and time). Other details may be included such as it being the first of a new series, a new programme etc. Long trailers often give the transmission day or time at the beginning and end.

Scripts

Promotion scripts are written in the same way as voice pieces and marked with suitable times to be read out. The presenter checks the wording before reading the script on air to avoid giving misleading times.

Recorded trailers

Greater impact can be achieved by pre-recording promotions using programme extracts, music and a tightly written script. The mood can be set with a suitable piece of music giving the trailer a definite pace, though the speech has to match the tempo of the music thus making it essential to work to split-second timings. In very punchy trails with music, automatic voice-over may be used to achieve swift fading down and up to fit the voice. Trailers need impact at both ends, this can be achieved by an attention-getting statement or music.

Playing trailers

Tape trailers are best transferred onto cartridges which are easier to handle. They should be labelled with title, duration, out words, and transmission or expiry date. Trailers which need introducing are accompanied by a script. The average duration of recorded promotions varies from 20 to approximately 60 seconds. When a programme is being heavily promoted several different trailers are produced to provide a variation.

Different versions may also be required to match the day or time, e.g. tomorrow, this weekend, tonight, etc., and this makes it important to label the cartridge correctly. A special rack is often set aside to hold all trail material.

When spare tape machines are unavailable trailers which are on reels may be played by attaching them to the beginning of programme tapes with just a small amount of leader left between the end of the trailer and the beginning of the programme. The tape is stopped at the end of the trailer, leaving the machine already threaded up for the next programme.

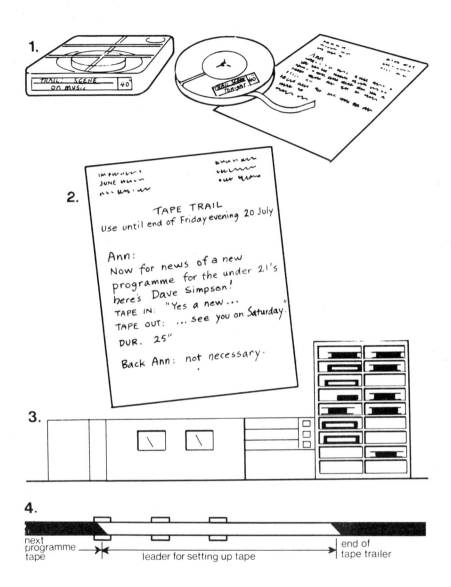

1.

2.

TAPE TRAIL
Use until end of Friday evening 20 July

Ann:
Now for news of a new
programme for the under 21's
here's Dave Simpson!
TAPE IN: "Yes a new ...
TAPE OUT: ... see you on Saturday."
DUR. 25"

Back Ann: not necessary.

3.

4.

next
programme
tape — leader for setting up tape → end of
tape trailer

PROMOTIONS

1. Programme trailers may be written and recorded using cartridges or reels.
2. Recorded trailers sometimes need introducing so cue sheets are left with
them giving transmission details and cues. 3. A rack is usually kept for holding all trail material. 4. Recorded trailers may be attached to the beginning or
end of programme tapes when separate machines are unavailable to play
them.

65

Events Diaries

All local radio stations receive a constant flow of requests from individuals and organizations for publicity. Providing the requests are quite legitimate, in good taste, and unconnected with commerce, a radio station can promote its own image both to the public and the groups concerned.

Daily list
One of the best ways of giving news of forthcoming events sent in by listeners is to provide a daily bulletin. Only the basic information is given in simple easy-to-read language including title, venue, day and time. Details of tickets are listed when needed. In this way an announcer or presenter can quickly scan the list and ad lib from one item to the next. Announcements may be grouped together in days or time of day, and sections e.g. jumble sales.

Packaged diaries
Diaries may be used for extracting items one at a time, or for presenting as a complete package. When a complete bulletin is read out, a light musical background sometimes helps, with the announcements read in a bright snappy style. An intimate informal approach is far better than presenting it as a kind of 'shopping list'. The majority of items listed are hardly likely to be hard hitting but they should be read with interest. The right music and delivery has to be chosen.

Compiling a diary
Once details of events have been checked and accepted they are filed for the appropriate day. Compilers sometimes check back with those sending in the news to confirm details. Many stations will only accept information sent in by letter so that details can be double checked. This also saves a considerable amount of secretarial time. Basic information is extracted from each postcard, letter or handout in the day's file. Station reception desks usually take a carbon copy of the events diary to help with listeners' enquiries.

Newsworthy items
Occasionally, items sent in to the events diary are of interest to the newsroom—in fact diaries are compiled by newsroom staff at many stations.

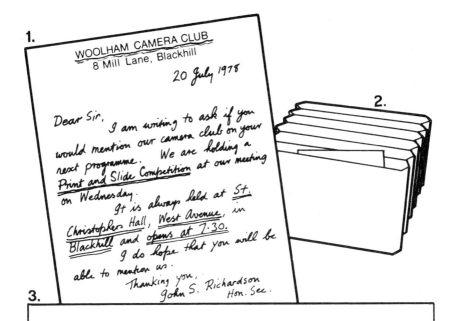

1.

WOOLHAM CAMERA CLUB
8 Mill Lane, Blackhill

20 July 1978

Dear Sir,
I am writing to ask if you would mention our camera club on your next programme. We are holding a <u>Print and Slide Competition</u> at our meeting on <u>Wednesday</u>.
It is always held at <u>St. Christophers Hall, West Avenue, in Blackhill</u> and <u>opens at 7.30</u>.
I do hope that you will be able to mention us.
Thanking you,
John S. Richardson
Hon. Sec.

2.

3.

WHERE & WHEN

Good morning,
And first news for the youngsters on holiday. The Bempton Childrens Play
Assn. present the Free Form Road Show, today, appearing at Daleside Advent-
ure Playground, Olive Road, Newtown, from 2.30 this afternoon.

Then, at Bempton Junior Library, there are Face Painting Sessions from 10
am to 4 pm. At Murton Junior Library, there's a Storytime Session for
the under 5's at 2.45 whilst at Megshill Road Junior Library, it's Storytime for the over 5's from 3 - 3.30.

Three films are being shown tonight at the Art Gallery, Civic Centre,
Newtown 'The Great Ice-cream Robbery', 'The Case of the Mukkinese Battle-
horn' and 'Encounters in the Dark', between 7.30 and 9.30.

Woolham Camera Club will be holding a Print and Slide Competition at their
meeting tonight at St. Christophers Hall, West Avenue, Blackhill, at 7.30.

Newtown Road Safety Committee meet at the Civic Centre at 2.30 this
afternoon.

EVENTS DIARIES
1. Example of request for information to be read out. Important details may
be picked out by underlining prior to typing the diary. 2. Requests may be
stored in separate files for each day until needed. 3. Part of a typed up events
diary with the basic details picked out. The announcer then 'reads around' to
make it sound more informal.

Self-operating

Programmes are either mixed by an operator in a control room or by the studio presenter or announcer. In local radio there is very little difference between control rooms and studios, since most of them contain control equipment for mixing, and microphones for presentation work. For complex programmes, with many inserts or microphones to balance, the mixing is performed in a separate control room whereas record shows using only one or two microphones and turntables are often operated by the disc jockey, with perhaps an operator to monitor the overall levels and quality in the master control room.

The presenter

Studio equipment is arranged around the presenter for ease of operation and includes facilities for playing records, tapes and cartridges. Programmes are mixed on a control board. Presenters wear headphones for receiving cues, taking level on sources and monitoring the programme. Whenever a microphone fader is opened the loudspeaker is automatically cut off thus making it essential that the presenter wears headphones. A presenter has to think quickly—whilst one record is being played on air, another disc or cartridge has to be lined up ready to follow it. If one source breaks down the presenter has to know immediately which other items may be used instead.

The presenter also has to liaise with other studios or remote sources. A typical programme might involve cueing and fading up a newsreader in another studio, talking to guests on other microphones, introducing reports from police or weather stations etc. When it would be too complicated for the presenter to play all the inserts an operator mixes the extra sources in a separate control room. One board simply acts as a sub-mixer for the other.

Operations

Turntables and cartridge machines are reasonably quiet when started but mains-operated tape machines tend to make a considerable noise. To avoid this noise, the microphone fader is closed before stopping or starting studio machines. Portable tape recorders make less noise but unless adapted will only take small reels.

Limiters and compressors help prevent accidental over-modulation of the programme and are used in some cases for compressing the presenter's voice (in the same way as pop music is compressed). A voice-over unit can also be linked to the controls for automatically fading down music to a background level during announcements.

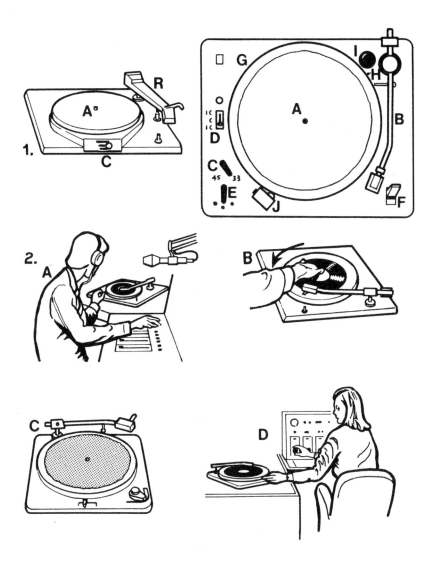

PLAYING DISCS
1. Examples of turntables
A, turntable with felt mat; B, pick-up arm; C, speed change control; D, local/ remote start switch; E, motor start and brake switch; F, pick-up raise/lower lever; G, guide markers for correct backtracking; H, stroboscopic markings; I, adaptor for records with wide centre hole; J, pick-up light.
2. Lining up a disc
A, the record is monitored from the mixer on pre-fade using headphones (or loudspeakers) and meter; B, the arm is returned to the beginning with the motor disengaged, and the disc carefully moved on to the start of the music. The disc is then backtracked by hand for part of a revolution. Turntables can usually be started by remote control from the mixer; C, older turntables are often fitted with loose slip mats and a brake—records being started locally by releasing the brake or grip of the felt mat (or record) with the turntable running underneath (D).

71

Record Care

Records are best stored loosely in vertical racks. Horizontal storing, one on top of another, and in hot areas warps them.

The library

Each record library has its own method of filing but, just as with books in a public library, they are all catalogued on cards. There is usually at least one alphabetical file of the entire stock by song or music title. Other files may be devoted to composers, artists, and types of music.

Stations which play a wide range of music file their records into specific categories e.g. country music, film, classical etc. Specialist music stations sometimes sub-divide a category still further. As soon as the library receives a new record, the track titles are noted on separate cards and the record assigned a reference number according to its place in the library e.g. FM0142 could mean position 142 in the film music section. Other cards may be made out to file in the artists tray etc. For convenience all 33 rpm and 45 rpm records are generally stored separately, because of the size difference, although there are exceptions.

Handling

The record grooves should never be handled because fingers always leave a mark behind which attracts dirt. The edges and label are used for handling, and a dust jacket and record sleeve replaced after use. At the end of a programme the records have to be carefully sorted out to match the correct covers otherwise wrong filing causes great difficulty for future users. In the studio, the records may be uncovered and stacked in order along a wire frame ready for use. Severe scratching and surface noise is created when uncovered records are left piled on top of each other.

Several proprietary cleaners are available but in extreme cases records may be wiped with methylated spirits and rinsed well in warm water, then dried with a soft smooth cloth moved around the disc. A note of badly worn tracks and other faults is made on the record sleeves. Sometimes a yellow wax pencil mark is drawn in a zig-zag fashion along the faulty track to prevent it from being played.

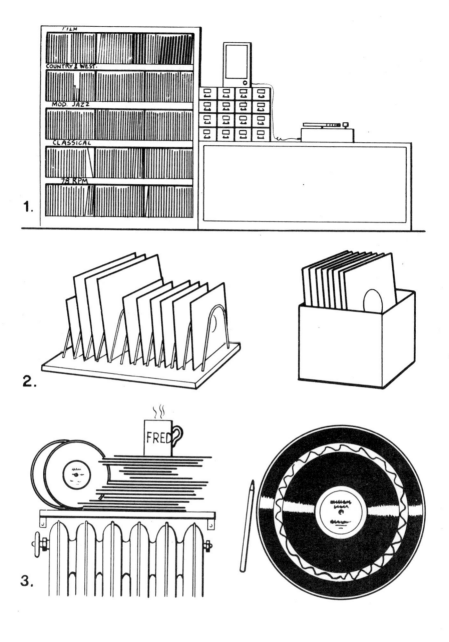

RECORD CARE

1. The record library. All discs and individual tracks are catalogued. Facilities usually include a record player. 2. In the studio. Records are best stacked neatly in wire record holders. Small wooden boxes may be used to hold singles. 3. Records soon deteriorate when exposed to heat and dirt. Stacking one on top of the other causes warping (and scratching when covers are left off). Records in wrong sleeves cause confusion. Badly scratched tracks not to be played may be marked with a wax pencil.

Record and Strip Programmes

Programmes may be completely controlled by the presenter or an operator depending on the programme's complexity. The presenter may have control over microphones, jingles and records with the operator mixing in tapes, telephones and outside lines.

Regular format

Sequence programmes have regular formats so that the listener knows what to expect at particular times. The presenter keeps as close as possible to a planned sequence of items i.e. fixed spots, including time checks, weather, news, events diaries, sport, women's items, shopping news etc., and even commercial breaks and kinds of music. Music may be planned with particular types played at certain points in the programme e.g. new releases, 'golden oldies', records in the charts etc. The actual choice of music may be left to the presenter or other production staff. Usually the presenter is designated as the producer (and very often, operator) of his own show as well.

Inserts and specialist spots

Sequence programmes use a considerable number of tapes for inserts. Short items of under two minutes are easily handled on cartridge (much longer items are more of a problem on cartridge because of the recycling time after pre-fading—unless a machine is used with rapid run-on). There is no doubting the advantage of cartridge machines because the presenter can play in all the inserts. Long tape inserts are kept on reels.

Short specialist spots within sequence programmes rarely have signature tunes because they tend to slow down the whole programme and give a hotch potch style of presentation when there are several inserts within one programme. Regular spots should always be short and interesting—remember, *it is far better to leave the listener wanting more: quality not quantity*!

Record requests

Most letters and cards are very difficult to read on air at first sight so most presenters prefer to either underline names and important parts, or copy them onto a script. Complete scripts are rarely used, mainly because there is just not enough time to prepare them and in any case would probably sound stilted.

Details can be picked out with coloured pens. Some programmes do not allow requests whilst others do, but even so it is not always possible to play exactly what is asked for.

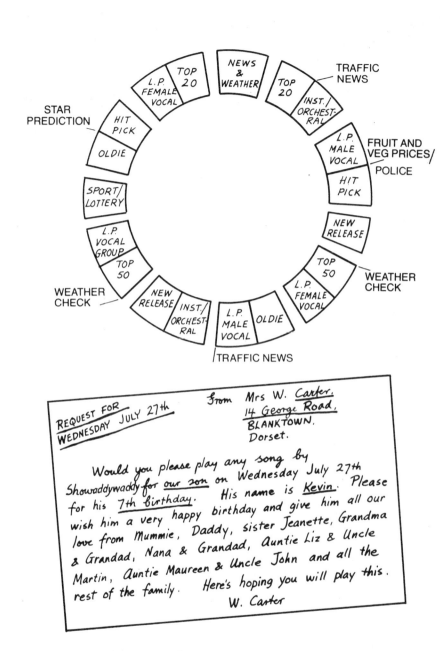

RECORD AND SEQUENCE PROPS

1. A programme sequence is much easier to follow when drawn out in the form of a clock. 2. Record request, underlined and ready for reading on-air.

Magazines

Local radio magazines cover majority to minority interests including programmes for women, sports fans, art lovers etc., and may be produced and presented by station staff or specialists in those fields.

Programme introductions

These invariably give some idea of the content although there are many different ways of introducing a programme including:

1. Straightforward use of a signature tune. The music is dipped after allowing time to establish itself, and the opening announcement made over the top. The music is then faded out gently to correspond with the end of the introduction. Music or voice can then easily follow it.

2. Fast signature tunes with several short musical phrases allow a much snappier approach. Automatic voice-over allows the presenter to 'jump in and out' of the music quickly rather than read continuously (as in 1).

3. Use of extracts. Short extracts from interviews, actuality etc., are sometimes played as a taste of what is to come. Each extract is linked briefly without giving away too much about the programme, and yet presented like a promotion (trail) to 'sell' it to the listener. The signature tune may be used throughout the introductory 'taster' or lost, once into the first extract.

This is then followed by an introduction to the first item. As the programme continues, the listener may be reminded of an item to be heard later in the programme and perhaps to keep pen and paper at hand to make a note of details, addresses etc. Magazines which are broadcast live first time round and then repeated from an ROT another day should not include time checks or references e.g. 'today', 'yesterday', 'tomorrow' etc., which would obviously be inaccurate if not edited out for the repeat transmission.

Magazines are usually rounded off at the end in the same way as they began using the signature tune with perhaps a mention of what will be in next week's programme. Signature tunes can be used to take up the slack when programme content runs short.

As an alternative to producing a complete magazine, items may be slotted individually within a strip programme. Whether producing a self-contained magazine or inserts for a strip it is important to work out the introduction needed for each piece, its duration, in and out words on tape etc., as well as a back announcement, if needed, and type the information on a cue sheet with a copy for the operator (see p. 78). Cue sheets should also accompany all recorded programmes (see p. 60).

WOMEN TODAY Thurs. 9. 6. 78.

RUNNING ORDER

CART. (RACK) — Sig. in (intro over)
TAPE — Exhibition
LIVE — Make-up
{CART A — Artist 2'50"
+
{DISC — (Seque S2 B3 go on handcue)
CART B — Do-it-yourself
CART(RACK) — Sig. out (prefade to 1059. 45)

1.

2.

TOPIC MAGAZINES

1. Running order for the operator of a local radio woman's magazine. Cues for starting tapes are taken from either scripts or the presenter (or both). Information is included for setting up discs and tapes. 2. Ways of introducing programmes. A, the signature tune is dipped whilst an introduction and menu is given, then the music is brought back up before dropping again for the first item. B, using automatic voice-over on a fast signature tune and 'jumping in and out' with the menu—the music being faded out manually as the first item is being introduced. C, Using a 'taster' or 'teaser', music may be kept running underneath.

Linking and Presenting

Links, or leads, into tapes give an outline of the topic, and tell the listener who is taking part, and often where or when, as well as giving official titles etc.

Sometimes it is necessary to use certain details from the beginning of a recording in the link but care must be taken to avoid the insert repeating what has just been said in the link. Tapes can be edited to avoid this repetition.

Cue sheets

Cue sheets are headed with the tape title, date, transmission time, and reporter's or writer's name. Further down it gives the studio introduction followed by the first and last few words on the tape and its duration. This is followed by a back-announcement if it is needed. The tape inserts, on reels or cartridges, are also labelled to correspond with the cue sheets. The operator and presenter each have copies of the cue sheets although when only one set of scripts or cue sheets is available the presenter may cue the operator to play the tapes with a hand signal. The operator, in turn, cues the presenter at the end of tapes by flashing a green cue light. Alternatively, the presenter may take a cue to start speaking at the end of a jingle or from the closing words of the tape (using the cue sheet out words as a guide). When people follow each other on the same microphone cues are given by hand from one speaker to the other. This also applies when a programme is being self-operated and the DJ hands over to a contributor sitting opposite, although there are many occasions when cues are unnecessary e.g. when a newsreader comes in on a jingle.

Back-announcing items

It helps after long interviews, to back-announce the interviewee and the subject. This gives a neat end to an item and forms a bridge before the next.

Pronunciation

Pronunciations are best checked before awkward names are broadcast. Place names can be checked with local sources e.g. police or the clergy, if station staff cannot help. When leaving a cue sheet for another presenter to read, awkward pronunciations should be written out phonetically.

Date

Title of story
and
name of writer

time to be
transmitted

the story or
introduction to tape

Tape in: "   _ _ _ _ _ "
Tape out: "_ _ _ _ _ _   "
Duration:
Back-announcement:

LINKING AND PRESENTING
Layout of cue sheet.

79

Documentaries

Radio documentary making involves many of the basic skills described in this book. A good documentary is well structured through careful research, planning, and production, all of which demand time and patience. It should have a good beginning and a good end—obtaining the listener's attention at the start and leaving them thinking as the programme finishes.

Research and planning involve:

1. Consulting experts, press cuttings, and textbooks etc., on the subject.
2. Making contacts and gathering background information.
3. Working out a rough structure for the programme.
4. Selecting sound archive material e.g. commentaries, famous speeches etc.
5. Choosing suitable music and sound effects on disc.

Production

After recording all the interviews and actuality, the first stage in production is to listen to all the material obtained and make notes.

Next, a rough running order is made out. It is at this stage that some material almost always has to be left out. The pieces required from all the recordings are assembled in the correct order by dubbing (see p. 144) using the notes. Music and sound effects on discs and studio inserts are best introduced later rather than dub them onto the compilation tape. All the tape inserts are separated by short pieces of yellow leader.

Once the inserts have been compiled in the set order, more intricate editing is involved to remove long pauses, fluffs etc. A rough idea of total programme duration can be estimated by adding together the timings for the inserts and speech and music links. Finally the programme is mixed by playing in the tape inserts from the compilation tape, records and studio links at appropriate points using a script, and recorded on a second tape machine. Any breaks for faulty operations have to be noted and edited out later.

Narration

Documentaries may be made with or without narration. The non-narrative technique (see p. 96) involves cutting out the interviewer's questions so that the subject tells its own story using only the interviewee's answers. Narration may be provided either by a studio link man after all the tape inserts have been assembled or recorded at the time of each interview or voice piece. Actuality i.e. sounds from events covered in the interviews, and suitable music all help to provide their own links, sometimes without further comment from a narrator.

SOME ASPECTS OF DOCUMENTARY MAKING

Researching.

Planning and making contacts.

Interviewing and recording actuality.

Obtaining music, sound effects discs, and archive material.

Listening to all the material.

Dubbing off in the correct order and editing.

Mixing and re-recording—the finished product!

Pre-fading and Timing

Most programmes have to begin and end at fixed times, especially if they lead up to a time signal or network junction. Programmes can be made to fill all available time until the set out point by:
1. Talking to time (or up to a short musical 'sting').
2. Fading out (if ending on music).
3. Pre-fading (dead-potting) i.e. starting a piece of music (on tape or disc) of known duration that time before the end of the programme, so that the music ends at the programme out time. The exception is on record programmes when music is pre-faded up to a fixed spot e.g. news, rather than the end of a programme. In this case the presenter should aim to use at least 2 minutes of the pre-faded disc on air.

Theme tunes

Two versions of a theme tune may be used: one with a short musical introduction for the beginning of the programme; and one with either a longer duration for pre-fading to time, or very short running time (a sting) to end on. Instrumental music is chosen because it is easier to make a smooth fade up and does not divert attention from the programme. Music may also be faded to time instead of being pre-faded providing it is started on air. *Music should always be started or ended cleanly on air—never faded at both ends*.

Theme tunes which regularly play programmes in and out are recorded onto tape for ease of lining up. It also prevents the wear and tear which a record would be subjected to each time. Cartridges are best for this purpose (see p. 44) because they are easier to set up.

Talk-over

When vocal music with an instrumental lead-in is played there is an opportunity to voice-over the music up to the singing. The duration of the lead-in is timed on a stopwatch and a note made of the timing on the running order. On transmission the stopwatch may be started at the same time as the disc although this is unnecessary if the introduction is rehearsed. Many experienced DJs do not use stopwatches as they are so familiar with the music, but until confidence and musical knowledge has been built up though, it is far safer to use a stopwatch. Mistiming sounds unprofessional, and over-use of the technique is very noticeable and irritating to many listeners. Talking-over is just one of the many skills a successful DJ uses. The same technique can also be used on purely instrumental music which, for example, builds up to a crescendo after 20 seconds or so. A variation of talk-over is to let the music establish itself for a moment and then dip the sound to voice-over.

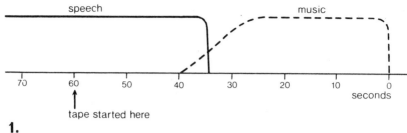

1.

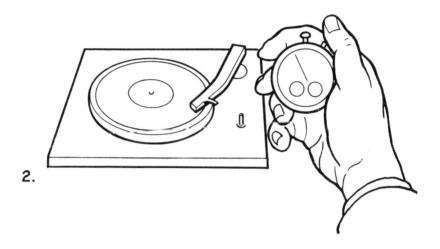

2.

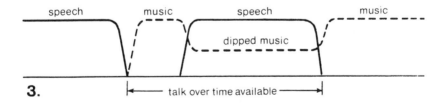

3. ← talk over time available →

PRE-FADING AND TIMING
1. Pre-fading a 1-minute signature tune to time means starting the tape 60 seconds to the end of the programme. It is slowly faded up on the closing words until fully faded up at the end of speech. 2. Finding the talk-over time of a disc. 3. Sometimes not all the talk-over time available is used. The music may be established straight after speech and then dipped for a further announcement a few seconds later before being faded up for the commencement of the vocal track.

Fades

Sound is always faded up or down in radio, and rarely keyed cleanly into a programme. The steepness of fade depends on the type of item or programme. Suitable points have to be found for fading music up or down. Fades can be used in different ways:

1. Cross-fade—fading up one source as another is faded out underneath. Unless this is done carefully it can sound very messy especially when music is in a different key.

2. Pre-fade (dead-pot)—starting a disc, cartridge or tape with a known duration that much time before the end of a sequence or programme, and fading it up only as the closing announcement is being made. This ensures that theme tunes or other musical items end to a set time, and is also called a dead or closed pot technique.

3. Segue—the clean butting together of music to music (or speech) without overlap as in cross-fades.

4. Pot-cut—the sudden closing of a fader to edit speech whilst on air. A knowledge of what is being said and a quick reaction are essential for stopping at a suitable point. What has been said must be sufficiently balanced editorially before further comment can be cut out. The fader must obviously be closed quickly and at the logical end of speech.

5. Down and up—when done slowly it can mark the passage of time.

6. Up or down-when joining a piece of music in the middle e.g. during a pre-faded sequence, it has to be 'edged' in by fading up. When leaving items before their natural end, they have to be faded out.

7. Edge in—some loud inserts and effects are improved by slight edging in i.e. starting at a slightly lower level and then quickly bringing up to the correct level.

A fade is said to be noticeable on medium wave when the level falls below 3 on a PPM.

FADES

Cross-fade
Introducing one source (B) as another (A) is faded out.

Pre-fade
The music is started at a pre-determined time before its end. Once the last item (A) has finished, and as the presenter (B) is ending, the music (C) is faded up.

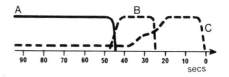

Segue
Music (B) following speech (A) may come in cleanly without a fade in and may be dipped after a few seconds to allow an announcement to be made over the top.

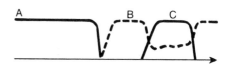

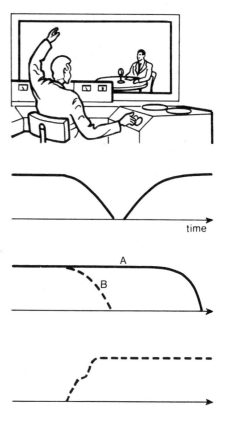

Pot-cut
A quick reaction and good editorial sense are required!

Down and up
A slow fade down and up can mark the passing of time.

Down (or up)
If a piece of music is longer than required (A) it may be faded out gently (B) before time. The fade has to fit the music to avoid sounding abrupt. Music may be faded up in the same way.

Edge in
Starting inserts at a slightly lower level and bringing them up to full volume.

85

Microphones

Certain microphones are equally sensitive to sound from all around whereas others are more sensitive to sound from particular angles. Microphones which have an all-round response are called omnidirectional, whilst those which are sensitive to the front and rear (but not to the sides) are bidirectional. Those able to select sound mainly from one direction only are unidirectional. The degree of sensitivity and the area they cover depends on their construction.

Types

The three basic types used for broadcasting are ribbon, moving coil and condenser. Ribbon microphones consist of a thin corregated metal foil diaphragm stretched between the poles of a magnet. As the foil vibrates, a voltage is produced. In moving coil microphones the output voltage or signal is produced by sound waves vibrating a diaphragm attached to the centre pole of a magnet. Condenser microphones work on the principle of varying capacitance between a diaphragm and backplate. To work, though, they need a power pack for applying a polarizing voltage between the two areas.

Response

In their basic forms, ribbon microphones are bidirectional and moving coil and condenser microphones omnidirectional. A cardioid (heart-shaped) response can be obtained by adapting any of these basic forms. Most cardioid microphones use either moving coils or condensers. Condenser microphones in this category usually have switchable responses controlled by varying the polarizing voltage.

Uses

Moving coil models are versatile robust microphones and ideal for reporting whereas ribbon types are far more delicate (with the exception of the lip microphone to be described later) and only used indoors. Indeed they are so sensitive they are never hand-held. They are used mainly for talks and interviews, and in music where sound separation is needed. Condenser microphones are the most expensive but give the best performance, and are available with omni – or variable responses. Cardioid microphones give good sound separation and are useful for music, announcing and DJ work.

	Moving coil	Ribbon	Condenser	Cardioid (condenser)
Approx. response varies according to model	omni	bi	variable or omni	uni
Handling	excellent	must be mounted	excellent but needs power unit	excellent
Outdoors	excellent but windshield required	unsuitable, wind affects ribbon	most are unsuitable for outdoor local radio work because they need a separate power unit	several are excellent but specifications should be checked first and used with a windshield
Noise & closeness	*must* be used close to speaker in noisy conditions as all round response, windshield needed	unsuitable for close work, bass increases when speaker nearer than 1–2 ft	suitable for close work	excellent in noisy conditions as greater sound separation, windshield needed
Uses	versatile, excellent for reporting	good quality studio microphone useful especially where sounds or acoustics need to be separated	high quality and versatile though usually more expensive	very popular for news reading, announcing and DJ work

Studio Interviews

Studio interviews may be balanced by an operator in the control room or self-operated (as in the case of DJ programmes).

Preparation

It is usual to invite guests who arrive whilst a self-operated programme is on the air, into the studio during a record or tape sequence. This way, any points about the interview (without going into details about the questions) and studio discipline (see p. 12) can be discussed whilst the studio microphone is faded out. Interviewees who are new to broadcasting need reassuring as to when they are 'on' and 'off' the air, so it is advisable to point out red lights and mention that when the loudspeaker cuts the microphone is live and is essential if the interview with the guest is to continue between records, or is made, for example, during a live news magazine. This helps prevent embarrassing moments—some people may get up immediately after an interview and even tear up papers in front of the microphone, without thinking that the microphone may still be live for further speech from the presenter!

Microphones

Self-operated programmes tend to use two cardioid microphones—one for the presenter and the other for a guest. This makes it easier to balance than using one microphone because level can be adjusted separately to compensate for a weak or a strong voice without the presenter having to alter his microphone position.

When an interview is balanced by an operator a single bi- or omnidirectional microphone may be used. Bidirectional microphones are very useful when only two voices are used. The person with the weaker voice is moved slightly nearer the microphone, or alternatively (to avoid the microphone 'popping' and bass tip-up) the stronger voice is moved further away, depending on studio acoustics. Any change in level of either voice during transmission has to be controlled by 'riding' the gain between voices.

Cueing inserts

Studio interviews in sequence programmes are sometimes illustrated e.g. an interview with a singer might be interrupted with one or two of the guest's songs on disc. This type of interview is considerably improved if particular cues can be arranged into the music e.g. going straight from a guest's comment into music:

'... Yes. That was my second song, and still my favourite,' followed by music. This is rather than an introduction from the presenter:

'Really. Well we've got that lined up on the turntable now, so here is ... ,' followed by music.

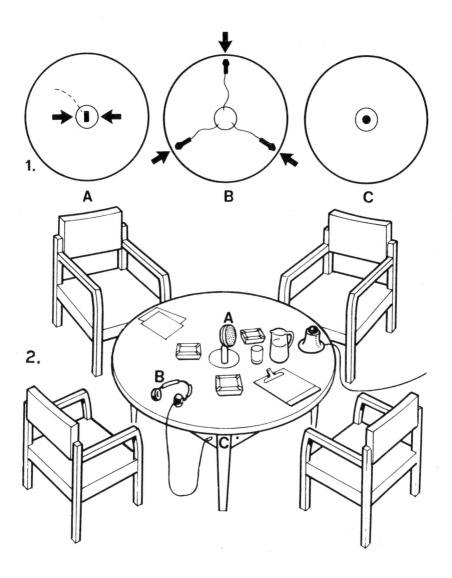

DISCUSSIONS
1. Microphones for discussions. Bidirectional microphones (A) are useful for face-to-face interviews, (interviewer and guest). Up to four people, two on each face of the microphone, may be easily accommodated, more than four is difficult. More people may be accommodated by allocating a separate cardioid or unidirectional microphone to each speaker (B) or using a single omnidirectional microphone (C).

2. Studio discussion table.
A, Microphone; B, headphones; C, separate headphone sockets for chairman and guests.

Interviews Outdoors

Wind noise is present on even the calmest days so for outside reporting a foam windscreen is fitted to the microphone, this will eliminate a lot of the noise but hardly affects the frequency response.

Holding the microphone

Some microphones used for reporting are omnidirectional which allow two or more voices to be picked up without moving the microphone too much. They cannot discriminate against background noise, so in noisy conditions they must be used closer to each speaker. Cardioid microphones may be used to avoid some of the noise. The microphone stem is gripped lightly between thumb and forefinger. Some microphones, and especially those with plastic cases, are susceptible to handling noise. A loop or two of slack cable is held to give extra freedom of movement and relieve the tension on the microphone connector.

The interview

For long and complex interviews names and brief details can be copied out onto small filing cards (which fit neatly in the pocket). Complete lists of questions are unnecessary, and in practice, regular news reporters rarely use notes.

The reporter discusses the outline with the interviewee without going into detail, this prevents the interviewee from preparing answers. A few easy preliminary questions allow voice level to be taken and put the guest at ease. Good priming questions which begin with: 'who, what, when, how, or why', have to be answered fully. It is important to listen to all the answers and follow up any question that is being evaded. It should always be made clear to the interviewee when the recording is in progress and his permission sought (preferably at the beginning of the recording). Avoid using interjections and exclamations, a nod of the head is all that is needed to give acknowledgement.

A close microphone technique is to be preferred to turning up the recording gain control on the tape recorder and also prevents one person speaking over the top of another to a certain extent. If someone makes a valid comment off the microphone, they are asked to repeat it with the microphone re-angled towards them.

If excessive noise develops during a recording, e.g. aircraft or trucks, it is better to stop until it has disappeared, and then retake that part of the interview. Background noise should be constant or at very low level throughout an interview otherwise jumps occur when the tape is edited. A few seconds of atmosphere are recorded at the end of each for use in editing. Unless working to a very tight schedule, it is better to record too much material than too little. Unwanted parts can always be edited out.

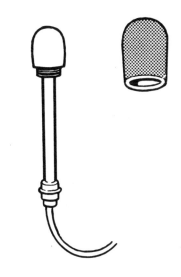

Foam windscreens are usually fitted to microphones used outdoors.

An equidistant microphone position is ideal for most situations—without having to move the microphone towards the speaker.

A close microphone technique is needed in noisy conditions, so the microphone is moved towards whoever is speaking.

93

Vox Pops

Various opinions can be collected from groups of people and broadcast to give the 'public' reaction to a topic. Alternatively the reactions of particular groups e.g. workers, shoppers, drivers etc., can be taken whenever there is news that affects them. Usually, several people are asked the same question and the replies edited together without the interviewer's voice each time. Although man-in-the-street interviews can reflect various opinions of a great many people they do not necessarily represent a fair cross-section of the public or group. Consequently, care is taken when editing them to try and balance the replies.

Recording opinions

Interviews are best recorded in areas where there are plenty of people. This saves time and ensures that background noise will be similar throughout the various recordings made.

A close microphone technique is used to reduce background noise. The microphone is pointed towards the interviewee throughout the recording, because all questions and necessary prompting can be cut out afterwards. Approximate level is taken first, remembering that it is better to slightly underrecord than overmodulate the tape causing distortion. A brief friendly approach is made to the interviewee giving the name of the radio station and seeking permission to record. At this stage, the recorder is set ready to record and held on pause, then released as the question is being asked. Key words in asking opinions are 'what, why and how.' They do not allow 'Yes' or 'No' replies, which could not be easily edited into a series of replies because their meaning would be lost.

The pause control can be used during long unusable or irrelevant replies. This saves tapes which can be used for more voices later, and at the same time allows the interviewee to continue talking—possibly leading to more constructive comments.

Editing

It is helpful to make a note of good comments at the time of recording so that points can be quickly picked out back at the studio. When all the answers have been monitored, the best are noted and copied onto another tape (dubbed) (see p. 144). The order of voices is best worked out before dubbing to reduce the amount of editing. Moving voices around often improves vox pops e.g. male and female voices are best split up to give better differentiation. Individual replies can sometimes be improved by splitting them up or using only the essential part of the answers. Intricate cutting (see p. 148) is then carried out if necessary to improve the flow of speech.

After the interview is completed, the original tape can then be bulk erased and re-issued as a splice free tape for use on portable recorders.

A test recording is made before interviewing to check the equipment and take rough level. Just before an interview the machine is switched to record and put on 'pause'.

When launching into the interview the pause control is released after a brief final check on level. The tape may be put back on pause during an interview if necessary.

At the studio the interviews or comments are dubbed in the order of transmission. An equalizer may be required and levels adjusted.

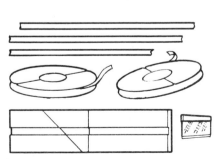

The tape is edited.

95

Interviewee Only

This technique is used mainly in documentaries and features and involves cutting out all questions and prompting.

Telling a story
By cutting out the interviewer's voice and skilful editing of the interviewee's voice it is possible to tell a story without any narration. A whole programme, in fact, can be assembled in this way by cutting in other voices whenever the first voice refers to other people. The approach is much more personal and intimate, but involves far more work than is ordinarily used in programme production.

Preparation
The style of editing has to be worked out before the interview, so that the interviewee can be guided in the right directions. All thoughts have to be connected, without the need for narration afterwards. As the interview is being recorded, the reporter or interviewer has to think how it will sound with the questions cut out—will the answers easily flow from one to the next, and are there enough cues built in to introduce other voices without the need for a narrator? Sometimes, the interviewee has to be asked to repeat or say something in a different way to provide editing points. Interviews where the reporter says very little except prompts are the best for editing. When all the material has been collected it is listened to from beginning to end and notes made with timings.

Dubbing and cutting
The recording notes are invaluable for quickly checking the contents of individual tapes especially when more than one voice is to be used. The required order is worked out for all the voices and the individual sections dubbed off in order and at the correct levels onto another reel of tape. When this is done the tape is in a rough edited form. Gaps and clicks caused through stopping and starting during dubbing are removed by editing. Smooth editing is then carried out to remove slight fluffs, and improve intelligibility. The problem is making the edits sound natural. The golden rule in tape editing is if it does not sound natural do not use it. Alternative cutting points can nearly always be found.

  When musical bridges or sound effects are required, the speech has to be banded onto a single reel, with yellow spacers between each section. The feature is then re-recorded onto another tape, with the yellow spacer used as stopping points whilst music or effects are introduced.

Only a microphone for the interviewer is required. The interviewer obtains the facts with the minimum of intrusion. The recording is listened to and notes made to help during editing.

The position of parts of the interview may be changed to restore the chronological order. Phrases may be cut out and labelled for editing back in later. Longer pieces have to be reeled.

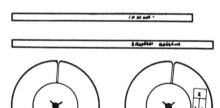

Fine editing is commenced once the tape has been assembled in the correct order. Pauses may be removed or inserted and other adjustments made to the flow of speech.

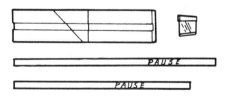

Portable Tape Recorders

There are two basic kinds of portable recorder: reel-to-reel and cassette machines.

Reel-to-reel
Reel-to-reel machines are by far the most widely used, they can work either on dry batteries or rechargeable cells. The common operating speed is 7½ inches per second with a half-track recording width. The other track is not usually used for mono broadcasting and news work because both tracks are played together on full-track machines. It can be useful in emergencies though when the machine runs out of tape because a recording can be made on the other track. The recordings then have to be played back on a half-track or stereo machine to separate them. Bulk-erased tape is used to ensure that the other track is free from previous recordings. Many portable recorders will not accept splices so edited tape cannot be used.

The controls are similar to those on a studio machine except that a pause control is usually incorporated which can be used on record. The advantages of reel-to-reel recordings are that they can be replayed immediately on studio machines, and edited straight away.

Cassette machines
Until recently cassette machines did not match up to the continued high performance of the professional reel-to-reel models though a few high quality models are now available. Until the advent of professional cassette machines the main criticism was that their frequency response was not good enough for broadcasting and that they could not stand up to rigorous daily use.

Under certain conditions even the cheapest of cassette machine can far outweigh reel-to-reel models in advantages. They are extremely light and useful in situations where a reel-to-reel machine would be too heavy or obtrusive. The main disadvantage, even with professional cassette machines, is that all material has to be dubbed off onto ¼ inch tape—cassette tapes are difficult to cue up and almost impossible to edit because of their slow speed and narrower width (though they can be spliced if damaged).

Domestic portable cassette recorders are very much cheaper but less reliable than professional and hi-fi models, sometimes a better microphone will give improved results. They are unsuitable for music but ideal where lightness comes before quality.

PORTABLE TAPE RECORDERS

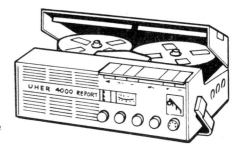

Professional reel-to-reel machine (mono).

Hi-fi portable stereo cassette recorder.

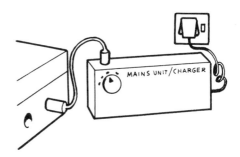

Machines using rechargeable batteries should always be put on charge after recording.

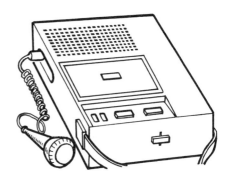

Domestic portable cassette recorder using torch batteries.

Outside Broadcast Vehicles

The two kinds of outside broadcast or remote vehicle used in British local radio are the radio car for interviews and small outside programmes, and control van for mixing more complicated programmes recorded on site or transmitted live.

Radio Car

Radio cars are basically estate cars or station wagons fitted with transmitting equipment and small sound mixers for sending interviews back to the radio station. The programme is transmitted back to base on UHF (though in some countries VHF is used) whilst cue and instructions are passed over a two-way VHF channel. The mixer can be used to take reporter's microphone, radio microphone, and a portable tape recorder as well as the output from more comprehensive mixing equipment. The apparatus is fitted in place of the front passenger seat. A 30 feet high pneumatic telescopic mast at the rear or through the roof carries a UHF aerial which, if it is of directional type is pointed towards the receiving aerial at the radio station for transmission. In built-up areas the receiving aerial is mounted on top of a tall building and the signal fed to the station via a music (land) line. Some receiving aerials may be rotated by remote control from the radio station to line up with the radio car's signal.

The two-way VHF link uses an ordinary car aerial mounted on the wing or roof.

Outside broadcast van

Many stations now have vans equipped with more comprehensive facilities for mixing complete programmes away from base. Facilities include studio tape recorders, mixer desk and monitoring equipment. Microphones can be linked to a multicore cable coupled to a connector on the side of the van. The output of the mixer is then fed to a tape recorder, UHF link transmitter, or music (land) line. Space is also provided for cable drums, microphones etc.

Outside broadcast vans used by local radio stations have a variety of purposes—one day a van might be used in the morning for a live disc show from a shopping complex and then go on to set up for an orchestral concert or perhaps a quiz or panel game in the evening.

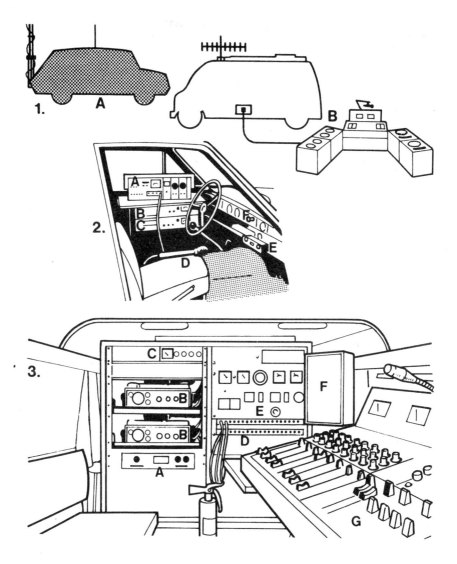

OB VEHICLES
1. A, Radio cars are used mainly for news and short programme inserts. B, Outside broadcast vans are used for more complicated programmes, either for live transmission or recording on site. Some are equipped with portable units for use away from the van. Multicore cables for interconnections help cut down the number of separate cables from equipment. 2. Radio car equipment includes A, small mixer and amplifier unit with sockets for microphone and tape machine etc.; B, UHF transmitter for the programme link; C, UHF receiver for radio microphone; D, reporter's microphone; E, two-way VHF radio to base for talkback and cue programme; F, keyswitch for pumping up aerial mast. 3. Outside broadcast van equipment may be built into portable units for use outside the van, or built-in according to the station's needs: A, transmitter, B, tape recorders; C, limiter/compressor; D, jackfield (patch panel); E, charging and power unit; F, monitor loudspeaker; G, mixer and control panel.

Radio Car

Studio centre staff are informed via the two way VHF radio when the car has arrived at the outside broadcast site and is ready for setting up. The aerial mast is raised by pumping up the pneumatic mast—though this is not always necessary when near to the station, with either a directional or omnidirectional aerial. Directional aerials are pointed roughly in the direction of the station's receiving aerial (which may be located away from the station centre). Omnidirectional aerials are not as good when used on the fringe of the car's transmission area, but are quick and easy to set up. Directional aerials have to be lined up with the base station. If a poor signal is obtained from the radio car, even after adjusting the aerials at both the radio car and base station, a new site has to be found. Sometimes just moving the car a few feet helps considerably though for any great distance the mast has to be lowered to prevent it tangling with overhead obstructions.

Lining up

High buildings, sports stadia, etc., as well as hills cause reflections and reduce signal level. Some industries are also a source of radio interference so the radio car has to be carefully sited away from such problems, yet giving the signal a clear path back to base. The strength of the radio car's signal can be checked at the station. Directional aerials at radio car and station ends are rotated so the station receives the highest signal strength possible with the minimum of noise and interference. Directional receiving aerials that are mounted on buildings or masts away from the station centre are rotated by remote control. Lines link the receiver to the station.

Cue

The reporter can receive cue programme from the station by listening on headphones (with the car loudspeaker turned off to prevent feedback on transmission) plugged into the two-way radio telephone. Immediately prior to transmission the station puts a feed of the on-air programme onto the radio talkback. In and out cues are arranged in advance with base so that in and out points are known. Tapes may also be played during a radio car transmission, either from the car or studio, and again, cues have to be pre-arranged for stopping and starting recorded inserts. An on-air handback to the studio is probably the safest end cue for short reports for news. At the end of the contribution the transmitter is switched off and equipment stowed away, with the mast lowered. The mixer equipment may also have to be put on charge back at base.

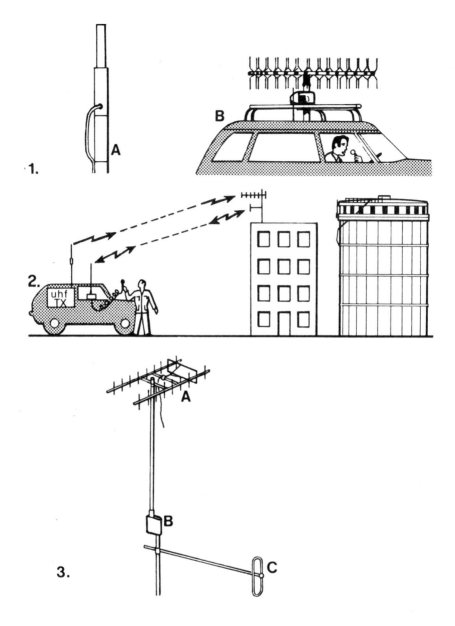

RADIO CAR TRANSMISSIONS

1. Radio car aerials may be either omnidirectional (A), or directional (B). 2. The studio staff and radio car operator line up the radio car and base aerials using the two-way VHF radio for talkback. Line of sight transmission gives best results, obstructions can affect the signal. 3. Remote control. Sometimes the receiving aerial for the radio station is some distance away. Remote control allows the receiver to be turned towards the radio car. A, UHF receiving aerial; B, aerial rotator; C, VHF aerial for two-way communication between car and base.

Radio Links

Inserts may be transmitted direct from the radio car to the radio station or over links using the car as just one stage in the transmission.

Radio microphones are commonly used to supplement the equipment found in the radio car, and may be used in places inaccessible with a vehicle. Used in this way, they can transmit back to base via a receiver and the more powerful transmitter in the radio car. Cue programme is provided on a lower quality two-way VHF radio. Two-way VHF radios can also be used for short programme inserts but tend to be on more crowded radio channels, and therefore unguarded against intrusion from other users—an important factor to be considered with live broadcasts.

Land line and radio car
When working outside the radio car's transmission area, contributions have to be sent back to base by other means. They can be recorded for replaying later from the radio station or nearest remote studio (down the line). Alternatively, the recording may be replayed from the radio car after driving it to within transmission distance of base.

It is also possible to install UHF receiving equipment at the end of the nearest land line linked to the radio station e.g. remote studio, sports stadia etc. Programme inserts can then be transmitted from the radio car to the UHF receiver at the remote studio and fed down the line to the radio station. In and out cues have to be worked out in advance and a feed of programme taken off-air unless the car's two way VHF radio will reach base.

Public radio telephone
In some countries radio telephones may be used with the public telephone system. These radio telephones simply transmit to a telephone exchange, from where the call is routed on normal exchange lines and equipment. By selecting the station number, a call can be routed through to a programme. The technical quality of the service is limited to the narrower frequency response of the public telephone system but is adequate for sports flashes etc.

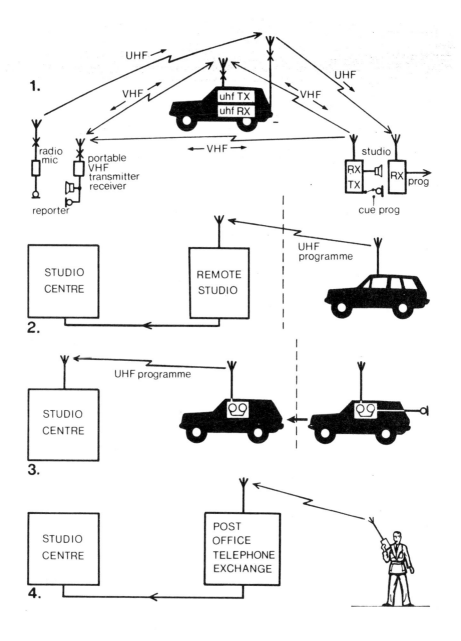

RADIO LINKS

1. Radio microphones and portable two-way radios free the reporter for live inserts from areas inaccessible by car. 2. Using a remote studio in the link when the studio centre is outside the car's transmission range. 3. Radio car used as recording unit out of normal UHF transmission range. After recording, the car is driven within transmission reach of the studio centre. 4. Using radio telephone through public telephone system.

Multiple Outside Broadcasts

Difficulties arise when a local station mounts a programme using several live outside broadcasts as in sports and election programmes. The operations have to be performed smoothly by a limited number of staff, and facilities provided to monitor one or all sources not on air.

The presenter
In complex live productions a presenter (anchor man) has to be aware of events second by second. He may need to monitor sources on headphones and have the facilities to fade up sources on air himself. On such occasions when there are mixers in both studio and separate control room, it can be arranged for the presenter to have control of microphones, tapes and records in the studio, with one or two sources available on faders for immediate use, and other sources and overall balance controlled by an operator in the control room. Leaving microphone control and one or two main sources on the studio board allows the presenter to make speedy decisions. Split feed headphones are useful for this purpose. One earpiece is used for cue programme and the other switched to sources as required.

The control room
The output of the studio board can be faded up on the control room mixer and balanced by an operator, with other sources as required. Alternatively, all mixing can be carried out by an operator using solely the control room board feeding the transmitter.

Talkback
Talkback to sports stadia and remote sites is often available on key switches on the control board.

In the normal position cue programme is passed to site. When the key is pressed the mixer talkback is routed to the OB.

Monitor loudspeakers can be left on OB lines so that control room staff can be immediately updated on scores, results etc. Stereo tape recorders with built in monitor speakers are useful for this as they permit simultaneous recording and monitoring of two lines.

Telephones may be connected direct to the site, for contacting reporters and giving cue programme. Circuits used for talkback purposes and cueing are called control lines (private lines, see p. 14).

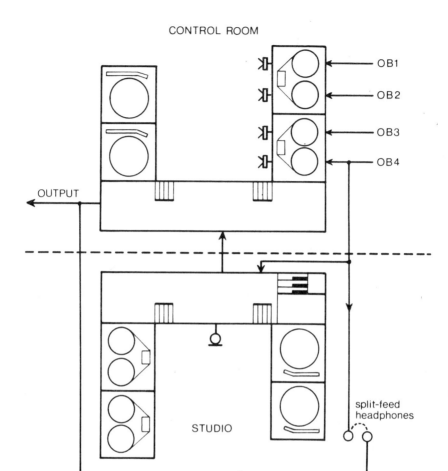

CONTROL ROOM

OB1
OB2
OB3
OB4

OUTPUT

split-feed
headphones

STUDIO

MULTIPLE OUTSIDE BROADCASTS
The presenter may use normal studio facilities and certain feeds of the OB
lines, with the mixer output fed to the control room where other sources may
be mixed in. Stereo tape recorders may be used for recording two commentaries simultaneously. Loudspeaker units can be plugged up for monitoring
each line. Split feed headphones allow the presenter to monitor two separate
outputs or feeds.

Remote Studios

Remote studios are usually unmanned and sited in main towns away from the radio station. They are linked to base by high quality land lines.

Apparatus

Basically, all that is needed is a small line sending amplifier and microphone, though other facilities are usually provided. Small portable mixers accept a microphone and tape recorder, this enables reporters to record or playback items locally without travelling several miles to the radio station. A small selection of adapters should be provided for connection with different portable tape machines. Cue is established either over an ordinary public telephone in the studio or separate control (private) line to base. In both cases, headphones may be plugged in, once contact has been established with base.

The room

Remote studios may be located almost anywhere away from noisy situations and are usually in public buildings. To keep costs down and because very little equipment is needed, remote studios tend to be small. Unfortunately, most do not have favourable dimensions for broadcasting and sound 'boxy'. The acoustics can be improved slightly by correct furnishing. Wall boxes, heavy carpets and curtains all help. Double glazing is essential when the studio is near to traffic or busy areas.

Operating

A close microphone technique reduces the amount of room colouration heard but the best position has to be found by experiment. A set of instructions in non-technical language is left on the table to instruct visitors on how to contact base and take level on themselves. A single main switch rather than individual ones powers all the equipment.

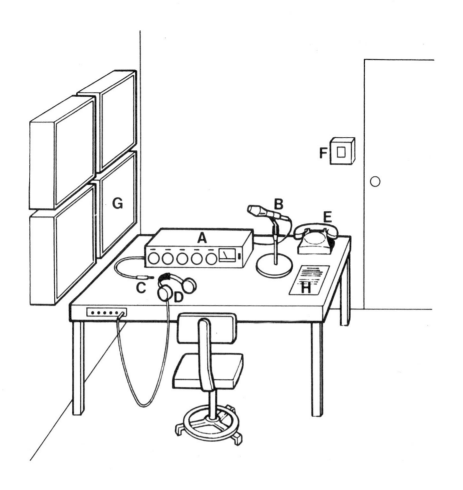

AN UNMANNED REMOTE STUDIO
A, mixer; B, microphone; C, lead and plug for portable tape recorder; D, headphones; E, telephone; F, power switch; G, acoustic boxes; H, instruction sheet.

Remote presentation

This is a form of presentation sometimes used in sports programmes. Presenting the programme from a sports stadium instead of the studio adds a sense of immediacy and reduces the number of handbacks. Good coordination between reporters and control room staff is needed to prevent operational mistakes.

The presenter
The presenter, or in this case the sports anchor, links the programme and usually provides reports and commentary from the sports stadium. From there, he can call in to reporters at other grounds for score flashes, and introduce recordings being played at the base station. Network sports services may also be used. The presenter listens to a feed of programme on headphones and when another source is being used and the microphone is faded out at the studio further instructions can be passed to the base on the commentator's microphone. A feed of network sport or other sources can be switched to the control line as required to help with cueing. A stand-by off-air receiver is provided in case the control line breaks down, or to listen to another station for information.

If cue programme disappears it does not necessarily mean there is a programme breakdown, so the presenter or commentator should continue until told to stop by staff at the station. Procedures are best worked out in advance for covering breakdowns.

Studio centre
The operator and presenter work from cue sheets or agreed instructions when replaying tapes. The operator informs the presenter when opening the microphone fader and also when it is safe to pass instructions i.e. when the microphone is faded out during other items. Normally, programme cue is sent on the control line to the sports stadium until the talkback key is pressed. Care has to be taken not to use this key or button when the presenter is using the line to monitor other sources including scores.

Other programmes and facilities
Similar conditions apply when a programme is being presented from a remote studio with limited facilities. It is possible to present a complete magazine programme including records without talkback (as in the case of loss of the control line) if both ends know the running order, in and out cues of items, and their durations.

Similar techniques are used with the radio car except of course the two-way radio is used for talkback instead of a control line.

110

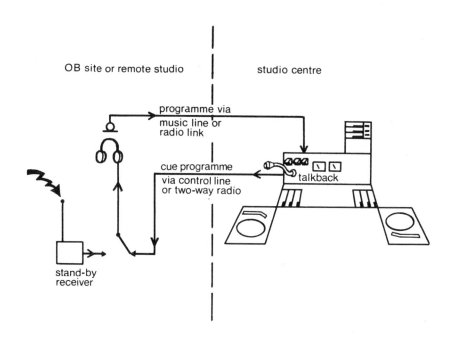

OB site or remote studio | studio centre

programme via
music line or
radio link

cue programme
via control line
or two-way radio

talkback

stand-by
receiver

REMOTE PRESENTATION
When programmes are presented from a remote studio or radio car, records
and tapes may be played in at the studio centre.

Commentator's Equipment

This usually comprises of a lip or close talking microphone, effects or background microphone, headphones, and reserve radio receiver, as well as a small amplifier or switching box. They can be used with a radio car or line-sending amplifier (line amp) connected by land line to the studio.

Lip microphones

Sports and outside events tend to be noisy occasions so noise-cancelling microphones are used to exclude background sound. The most popular type uses a ribbon and unlike its studio counterpart is extremely robust. It can be used fairly close to the mouth, the actual distance being set by a mouth guard. The advantage of a lip microphone is it excludes much of the noisy atmosphere, without any need for the commentator to be in a separate box (which would sound boomy and unlike a sports stadium). The disadvantage is that it cannot easily be used for interviewing. A second lip microphone is best for interviewees.

Effects microphones

Lip microphones exclude so much of the background that crowd effects have to be mixed back in to make the commentary sound more realistic. An omnidirectional microphone is used to pick up crowd noise. This can then be balanced to a suitable level against the commentator's voice.

Controls

The radio car is used for covering events from sites used only occasionally and also when the commentator may have to be mobile. On other occasions land lines are used to provide high quality circuits for commentary and a lower quality one for talkback (control line). In Britain these are booked as music and control lines from the Post Office. An ordinary public telephone line with a headphone attachment may be used instead of a control line. The commentator is provided with a line-sending amplifier or mixer for the microphone. Headphones are connected to the control line or telephone. The actual design differs from station to station. In their most elaborate form they may be combined in a case with switches for automatically controlling the crowd noise when an effects microphone is used. The simplest unit consists of a small battery-powered amplifier which plugs into the OB line.

Preparation

Lines are checked in advance by engineers but local radio commentators often arrive early to line up with the studio and check equipment. It is useful to know where the nearest telephone is in case of total breakdown. Some commentator's boxes include a reserve receiver so that if the control line is lost during transmission cues can still be taken off air.

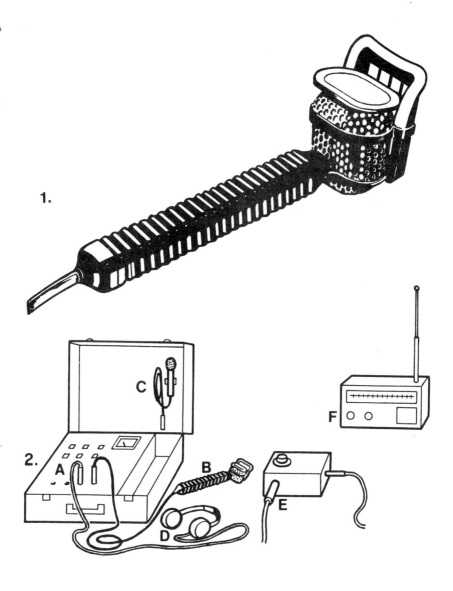

COMMENTATOR'S EQUIPMENT
1. Commentator's lip microphone used with either radio car equipment or portable units for sending by line. 2. Equipment for commentating varies from fully equipped suitcases, holding A, amplifier unit; B, lip microphone; C, effects microphone; and D, headphones, to much simplified line amplifiers for just the lip microphone. Some units include portable receivers so pro-gramme may be received off-air if the control line fails.

Commentating

The outside broadcast commentator is a specialist. Most local sports commentators are on very good terms with the teams they follow and build up an immense knowledge of sport in the area. A commentator researches his material beforehand and in the case of sport, makes enquiries about the opposition as well as the home team. Basic information on successes, failures, injuries, new players, disputes and transfers etc., all help to provide a steady foundation. At other events, the commentator does as much reading and talking to officials as possible before the transmission day.

Notes

Although commentating is essentially ad libbing, a set of notes are invaluable for jogging the memory or providing extra information during lulls in activity. These can be put on separate cards to form a small index which can be opened quickly as required. A programme is essential and this is best placed on a clipboard to stop it blowing away. Few programmes are completely accurate by the time of the event so a last minute check is made on names and positions. An introduction can be written in advance and late alterations written in as they are received.

Setting the scene

The listener has to be positioned for the action so the commentator describes the general scene first e.g. the kind of day, the size of the crowd etc., and works up to the details, although he may well introduce it with a headline about why it is so special or important implications e.g. a relegation battle, if it is not already covered in the studio hand-over. Before action commences the commentator gives positions—to the left, to the right etc., and colours or other relevant details.

Action and cues

From time to time the listener has to be reminded of some of the basic facts and, in sport, of the score and time. These are easily mentioned during the lulls, though the commentator is always ready to finish quickly what he is saying and pick up any sudden action. Marks are made on the programme to show scores, timings, etc., so that brief summaries or reports can easily be made. For this purpose, it can be useful to attach a stopwatch to the clipboard. Once underway, the commentator should carry on until told to return to the studio.

COMMENTATING
1. Set the scene: the spectators, weather, the team, etc. 2. The club programme, stopwatch and other notes may be attached to a clipboard, with
papers held in place at the bottom with a rubber band. 3. Keep the listeners
informed and break off to describe the unexpected.

Sports Reports

Sports reports and flashes are sent in via a variety of sources: radio car, remote studio, land line, and telephone.

Flashes

These are usually short up-dates on the score and scorers, with brief details. They form part of a pattern where a sports programme fades up reporters in turn for the latest news. The first piece of essential news, therefore, is whether the score has changed and what it is. Next comes the scorers, times, and details. By trimming down to bare facts, the reporter can condense the information to under 15 seconds and still find time to repeat the score at the end. It sounds better to end on the score or punch line, which act as reminders, rather than simply return to the studio. A whole series of hand-backs sounds repetitive and the practice at some stations is to do away with them. A reporter also sounds more knowledgable (and part of the programme) if he can occasionally pick up comments or phrases used by the studio link-man, or reporters at other sports grounds, to offer a contradiction or confirmation e.g. 'Well no score here either, but ... '.

Correspondent's Reports

Reports can be of almost any duration ranging from short half-time summaries to almost feature length items with extracts from recorded commentary. When reports are being recorded for use much later, or repeated the following day, reference to the day and time are left out. Game reporters write out their final report as the game is in progress so that on the final whistle they are ready to immediately reflect on the whole game. Some prefer to make brief notes—the choice is very much a personal one depending on the reporters ability to ad lib, and the pace or style required by the station. Reports that are being recorded are monitored off tape by an operator so that any mistakes or faults can be corrected before the reporter leaves the stadium.

Highlights from commentaries can also be linked with reports. As the game is in progress, the studio records the whole commentary, whether faded up on air or not. Whenever a player scores, the tape position is noted. These sections are then dubbed off in order onto another reel or cartridge. This system works well for other types of outside broadcasts including election programmes. As one tape machine is taken out of service to dub off a result another recorder is set running so that further action is not missed.

Alternatively, the dubbing operation can be left until the end but this obviously delays the production of the package. The tape counter is used to locate the position of extracts needed. Changes in sound even during high speed reeling can tell an operator the location of items e.g. crowd cheering.

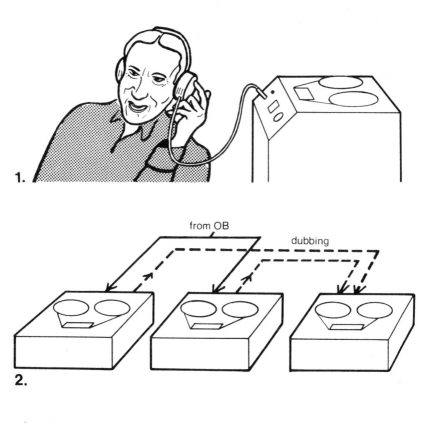

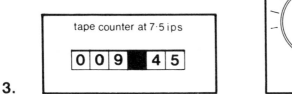 

SPORTS REPORTS
1. Monitor reports off tape as they are being recorded so that faults are noticed immediately. 2. Three tape machines are needed for dubbing off extracts whilst commentary is in progress. After dubbing the second recorder may be used for recording commentary whilst more extracts are dubbed off the first machine. 3. The tape counter is used to locate extracts.

Telephone Inserts

Telephone inserts i.e. voice pieces and interviews are used only when material cannot be sent quickly by other means. Consequently their use tends to be limited to news and sport. Other topics lose their effect when sent by telephone because of the lack of immediacy. Allowances have to be made for telephone quality i.e. a much more restricted frequency range than the broadcasting system, and telephonic noise. Inserts are kept as short as possible, preferably being no longer than 2½ minutes depending on the line. When the call is being set up a check is made on quality. If the line is a bad one, very often a better one can be found by redialling.

Dialling a call direct is to be preferred to operator-assisted calls because there is less danger of accidental intrusion. Obviously if another person breaks into a live call, it has to be wound up immediately. The operator should be asked to remove all timing pips. If this service is not asked for, and the pips are heard during a recording, the reporter should pause for a moment and retake his last line. It is helpful sometimes to repeat vital information after a call e.g. 'So that 3–1 win puts United back on top.'

Lining up
When a reporter rings in to the control room (usually an unlisted number) the call is checked for level. Next, if it is to be recorded, a tape is set up to record on and the reporter told when to start e.g. 5 from now (5 seconds). This gives the studio operator time to put the phone down or mute the handset's mouthpiece. The tape should be listened to as it is being recorded so that if there is any fault it can be retaken immediately.

When contributing to a programme as it is being produced i.e. live or recorded, a clean feed of the programme provides programme cues. Clean feed is a feed of the programme without the contributor's voice. Telephone balancing units (equalizers) are located in the master control room apparatus bays.

The telephone is also used in a similar way to interview people with the reporter's voice being of studio quality. The interviewee should be made aware that he is about to be recorded or broadcast and his permission sought (preferably on tape).

Studio to studio
One station may be linked to another by telephone line for sending news tapes. This is the next best thing when a music line or radio link is unavailable and offers slightly better quality than over an ordinary telephone handset. Studio mixers and telephone balancing units allow a direct connection to the line at both ends (see Contribution p. 132).

1.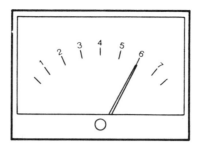

2.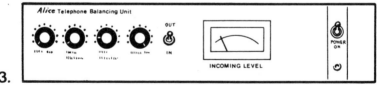

3.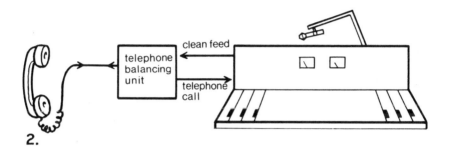

TELEPHONE INSERTS

1. Telephone calls should be peaked higher than on normal speech—around 6 on a PPM. 2. A clean feed i.e. without the telephone line, of the mixer output is fed to the caller during phone-ins and other telephone interviews. 3. Many telephone balancing units allow adjustments to be made to the quality of broadcast telephone calls.

Phone-ins

Most stations have special arrangements to avoid the public telephone exchange becoming jammed with listeners' calls during a phone-in. Normally, particular numbers are allocated for these programmes, so that other calls can be made in and out on the usual station lines. Control rooms and studios equipped for phone-ins have a keyswitch unit for answering the calls, holding, and feeding into the mixer. Calls can be assigned to particular telephone balancing units in turn. The units themselves may be linked to separate mixer channels or to a rotary selector connected to one channel. The actual method of switching varies from station to station but the principle of routing calls remains the same.

Prior to broadcast

Station policy at some studios dictates that the caller should be re-called from the studio on an unlisted number after obtaining the name, number and details of the call. This has the advantage of freeing lines quickly for other callers. When a call is finally routed to the mixer it is checked for level and quality. The caller is asked to speak clearly and loudly (though not shouting) and also to turn off, or turn down his radio set so it cannot be heard at the telephone. Failure to do this causes a feedback on a live programme. Next the caller is given a clean feed of the programme and asked if it is loud enough. From this point onwards, the caller is left with clean feed until being faded up so it is courteous to say there will be a pause until going on air and not to hang up. If the caller has been kept waiting for any length of time, an apology should be made for the delay.

When several calls are being lined up simultaneously, it is not always possible to give clean feed to them until just before being faded up so callers should be warned they will hear nothing for a while.

Precautions

If a call becomes unintelligible or someone else can be heard (even in the distance) it should be wound up, and a follow up call made to the caller.

To prevent profanity being broadcast, the programme can be delayed for a few seconds on a tape loop, before being sent to the transmitter. A delay of about 7 seconds is all that is needed for an announcer to censor remarks. When a programme using a loop is about to be broadcast a jingle or pre-recorded announcement, the same length as the tape loop, is used to cover the initial delay. This is played direct without the loop, at the same time as the programme begins. As the jingle ends, a switchover is made to the tape loop. As a final check on programmes, a recording is kept of the transmissions.

This is easily obtained, if, instead of using a loop the delay is obtained by recording on a reel of tape on one machine and replaying it on another.

120

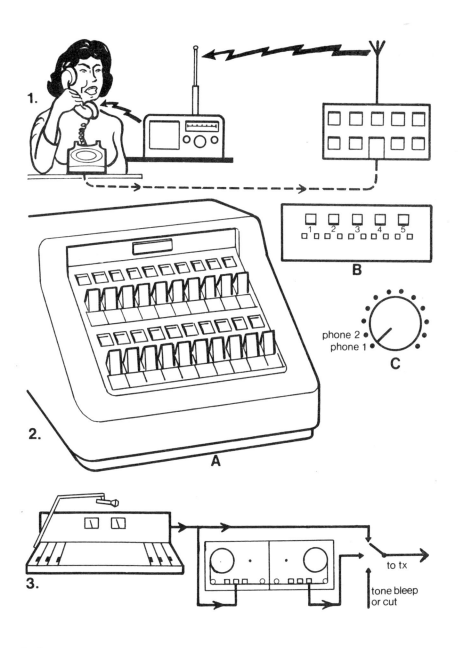

PHONE-INS

1. Feedback occurs when an on-air caller has his radio on. 2. Studio calls may be switched through to the desk using a small switchboard (A). Keyswitch positions allow the operator to speak to the caller or route the call to the mixer, via pushbuttons (B), or multiway switches (C) linked to a fader module, and telephone balancing equipment. 3. The programme may be delayed by a few seconds to give time for cutting out profanity, using a censor key.

Voice Pieces

These are used by almost all kinds of factual programmes and are written and read by the reporter working on the story either from the studio or from the scene.

Scripting

Voice pieces can be completely scripted or partly ad libbed. When ad libbing it is best to have the introduction and ending worked out in advance with notes as a guide. In any case, a good voice piece (or report) should sound natural. Try reading it aloud first. To ensure fluff-free delivery, scripts should be either handwritten clearly or typed with double spacing. Some reporters dictate their pieces to a typist. Timing may be based on a delivery speed of 180 words per minute (three words a second) or faster.

A voice piece should:

1. Sound natural.
2. Be logical.
3. Be easy to understand—with short rather than long sentences.
4. Have a definite beginning and end.
5. Be direct e.g. 'You may ... ' rather than 'Listeners may like to know ... '.
6. Avoid stringing too many adjectives together.
7. Avoid highly technical expressions which are difficult to follow.
8. Use Christian names instead of initials.
9. Be written in colloquial style i.e. English as it is spoken rather than written, e.g. 'I've' for I have etc.
10. Be well punctuated to aid delivery.

Reading

As with interviews, the beginning of the voice piece should not repeat what is said in the lead-in. It is helpful to offer the producer or editor a lead-in which fits the voice piece.

Fluffs and repeats made during the recording of a voice piece are noted on the script for use in editing later. Recorded voice pieces should always be listened to after editing to check that all double takes have been removed. A copy of the voice piece script usually accompanies the tape to help studio operations.

VOICE PIECES
1. Dictating the story to a typist can help ensure the voice piece flows. 2. Write for the listener—not the reader. 3. Listen to the tape after editing out fluffs in case one has been left in!

Scripts

The style of writing for radio is more direct than for the press. Only a relatively short time is allocated to each story compared with the space a newspaper would give. Consequently facts have to be condensed and simplified so that the listener understands first time. This applies as much to continuity and promotional material as to news and sport.

Scripts should be:

1. Clear and concise.
2. Immediate (with reference to the time of day if it is known when the piece will be broadcast).
3. Uncomplicated.
4. Easy to understand with analogies if necessary.
5. As brief as possible.
6. Fluent—a script should never sound like text. A good announcer can make the best of a bad script but consistently good reading depends upon the 'flow' of the script.
7. Consistent in style with the studio's normal way of presenting, and also from script to script.
8. Typed on separate sheets.
9. Avoid running sentences onto following pages.

To help the listener gain as much out of a story as possible, essential information is left out of the opening part of the lead sentence.

The first part may be attention getting and leads onto details later. When stories with similar topics follow each other the second one can lead on from the first e.g. '. . . still with fishing and . . .'. There is a limit to how many times this can be used within one programme.

Layout

As with lead-ins and voice pieces, the script is marked out with the date and time of transmission, writer's name, and programme or story title. If the script is an introduction to an insert, further details are listed including the in and out words, and duration of the insert. The page may also have a mark to show it was from an external source to be credited, or if it has been rewritten.

Some script paper has edge markings to show approximate durations. Scripts are typewritten with double spacing and wide margins. Mistakes are best crossed out by pen than individually on the typewriter. Heavily corrected scripts are better retyped. Single words can be corrected by crossing out and writing the word above. Scripts are easier to read when each sentence is indented as in the beginning of a new paragraph.

1.

NEWS   June 17 1977

17.30   RUNNING ORDER

1. John, headlines
2. David, news (separate running order)
3. John — trail part 2.
4. Commercial break
5. John cues police cart 60
   out — "... where Lesley is".
6. John, weather.
7. John cues Alan & Chris with sport

Chris cues David with 18.00 news
(separate running order)

CARTS
J, 28, 26, 27, 21, 19, G, K, C, E, F, H
60

2.

YORK REPORT   June 17, 1977

12.45   RUNNING ORDER

1. HEADLINES
2. FIRE — Mike live radio car
3. MURDER — Paul/Insp. Jackson 2'15".
4. NEWS — Jim
5. GYPSIES { i. actuality 10"
            ii. vox pop 20"
            iii. residents 2'30"
            + actuality at end
6. HOUSING — Nigel live V.p. council studio
   * May be earlier if poss.
7. WEATHER — Charles.

DIFFERENT STYLES OF NEWS PROGRAMMES
1. Typical running order for news magazine on a commercial radio station combining local and national news. Numbers and letters along the bottom indicate the order of recorded inserts on cartridges. The 'news' segment includes national and local material—often with inserts on cartridges.
2. Type of running order for a local news magazine. The actual 'news' segment within the programme would normally include short bulletin items rather than inserts—which may be from a variety of sources.

Networks

When a station can in some cases draw upon items or programmes from a national service which may either be transmitted nationally or sent by land line to each local station. A programme can therefore be broadcast simultaneously (SBD simulcast) by several different local stations. The most common form of simulcasting is for national news where local stations take a feed of a nationally read news bulletin. Items may also be recorded from network for use later. Some systems use a multipurpose distribution line (see p. 130) switched centrally to any of a number of sources. The problem with programmes broadcasted simultaneously in countries with different time zones is suiting national programmes to local times. One method which can be used is to record national programmes locally from the line and replay them at more suitable times.

Opting

Programmes have to run to time when the station joins network at fixed times. This can be accommodated either by pre-fading music to time (see p. 82) or using live announcements prior to joining network so that timing differences can be absorbed.

If an organization permits its local stations to join or leave network programmes as they wish, the problem of joining neatly arises. It is much tidier to join at the beginning. Linking into the middle of speech is avoided except during sports commentary. If a record programme for example is in progress on network it is much better to join it on music, if necessary by using programme information or records to shorten or expand a junction. The announcer listens on headphones to network at the same time as announcing locally. Stations using a national service at precise times have little difficulty in joining network. All local music and speech has to end promptly before 5 seconds to the hour when taking the Greenwich Time Signal (GTS) to avoid any overlap onto the pips. There are 6 GTS pips, the last one marking the actual time, e.g. one o'clock. Network is pre-faded first for level and to know when it is clean i.e. silent, and the right moment to join, otherwise there is always the possibility of broadcasting the tail end of music or speech from the national service before the pips.

Rebroadcasting

Programmes are either taken off-air from the national transmission or from the land line. Medium wave transmissions are of insufficient quality for rebroadcasting so line feeds must be used when VHF is unavailable. The network feed is routed through the equipment room and onto the master control board where it can be mixed. Some mixer channels are specially assigned to network feeds whereas others have multiway switches or a switching matrix fitted so a number of sources can be accepted on one channel.

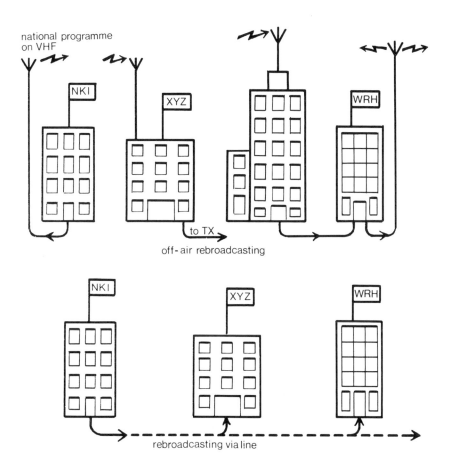

national programme
on VHF

NKI

XYZ

WRH

to TX

off-air rebroadcasting

NKI

XYZ

WRH

rebroadcasting via line

NETWORKS
Network programmes may be received either from VHF transmission or by line, allowing any number of stations within the organization to broadcast items simultaneously from their own transmitters.

Distribution

A line distribution system may be used for carrying a variety of sources throughout the day, including network programmes (see p. 128), national news, interviews, etc. The line is switched centrally at the station supplying all the services.

News

National news can be rebroadcast from the network or read locally using interviews supplied in advance on the line from the national service. Local stations supplied by a national news room are continually updated by teleprinter on news stories and distribution circuit details. Cue information for individual tapes may be sent by teleprinter or read over the line. A distribution circuit used primarily for news might be used most of the time for sending interviews which stations can rerecord for use in their own news programmes, and the rest of the time switched to a studio for giving half-hourly or hourly news bulletins. The actual use of network and distribution lines varies from organization to organization.

Programme services

Distribution circuits may be used for sending inserts or complete programmes to individual stations thus national programme services can supply information of particular interest to local stations.

Recording

Tape machines are allocated at each station taking distribution feeds, for recording off the line. News interviews tend to be short i.e. under 2 minutes and easily transferred to cartridge. Longer items have to be recorded on reel-to-reel machines. National news services generally begin with a verbal rundown of items on the circuit (as a check against lists sent by teleprinter) and then gives cue material unless this has been sent by teleprinter. Reel-to-reel machines are generally used when cue material is sent verbally by line, so that the script can be typed up later. The national service warns when a tape is about to be played and gives a count-down e.g. 'Going in 3, 2, 1.'

Syndicated tapes

Some studios and organizations duplicate programmes. These syndicated tapes are produced by government departments, commercial interests and disc jockeys, as well as broadcasting organizations. A duplicate of a programme may be sent to each station by mail, or the master tape sent to the central service for reproduction on the distribution circuit.

130

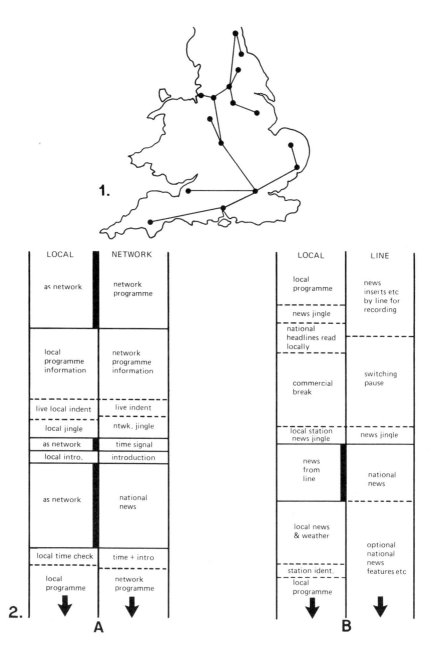

1.

LOCAL	NETWORK
as network	network programme
local programme information	network programme information
live local indent	live indent
local jingle	ntwk. jingle
as network	time signal
local intro.	introduction
as network	national news
local time check	time + intro
local programme	network programme

A

LOCAL	LINE
local programme	news inserts etc by line for recording
news jingle	
national headlines read locally	
commercial break	switching pause
local station news jingle	news jingle
news from line	national news
local news & weather	optional national news features etc
station ident.	
local programme	

B

2.

DISTRIBUTION
Part of a typical distribution system. A national programme service may be fed directly from Post Office centres or via other stations depending on the organization. 2. Examples of junctions and breaks encountered using a national news service from a network (A) or a line system (B).

Contribution

Many local radio items are of interest to other areas if not the whole country. Some stations have facilities for sending material to other stations. This may be done in several ways. News items may be sent by teleprinter or telephone and read locally (a telephone report can be broadcast as well), or land line. Interviews and features which are required the same day are sent by land line. A circuit is booked from the sending studio to the receiving studio and the item either sent live or replayed on a tape machine. At the receiving end, the item may be broadcast live or recorded for use later. Local items may be sent to the central service for use in nationally broadcast programmes or for distribution to other stations. An alternative to using distribution circuits is to send items via the public telephone system using studio mixing equipment if possible at each end to improve the limited frequency range of the telephone line.

Facilities
Some stations have studios set aside for contributing to network programmes whilst others have to make do with sending reports by telephone line. A small studio may be specifically used for news contributions, consisting of a microphone and tape machine connected to a mixer linked to the line. Talkback (control) is sent via the public telephone system.

Sending material
When a line has been booked, the control room of the receiving studio is telephoned prior to the arranged time. Line-up tone is sent to establish the connection and that it is in working order. It is usual to break the tone momentarily at an agreed moment to confirm it is the correct line. The telephone is often used for control purposes between sender and receiver, and may be connected to a pair of headphones for ease of working. At the receiving station a tape is set up to record on and the sender told to start. Before sending the tape or voice piece, the sender first identifies himself and gives cue material and pronunciations etc. When replaying tapes the sender has to switch off the microphone before starting the machine to avoid studio noise and acoustics being recorded at the receiving studio. At the end of sending a recorded item the sender confirms that the contribution has finished or that there is more to follow. Before starting it is also a good idea to give the duration of the piece so that the other station or studio does not run out of tape half way through. A good starting cue for material is to say, for example, 'Going in 5,4,3,2,1'. The receiving studio then cuts off the cue material from the tape (after typing it up) and prepares it for transmission or redistribution.

132

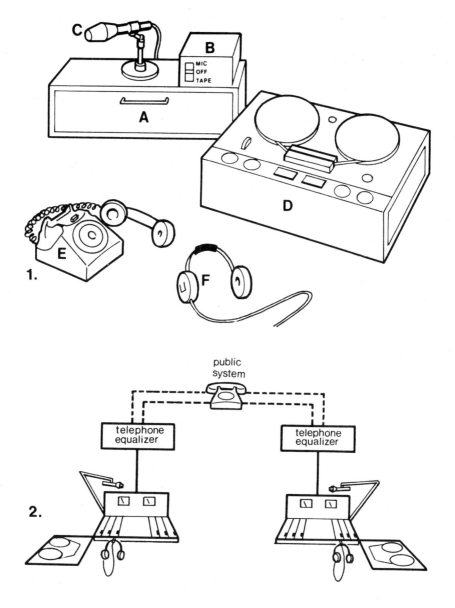

CONTRIBUTION

1. Contribution equipment comprising of A, automatic control unit; B, switching box for putting either microphone or tape machine to line; C, microphone; D, tape machine; E, telephone for lining up and receiving talkback—with a socket so that headphones (F) may be used. 2. Programme material may also be sent from station to station by telephone line using studio equipment linked to equalizers. Studio microphone and headphones are used. They may also be used for talkback by either station prior to, and after, sending material.

Recording and Rehearsal

A check is obviously made to see that all equipment is working normally before beginning a programme. If the studio has just been used for another programme the chances are that it will already have been lined up. A standard level of tone is used as a reference when adjusting equipment. This should read 4 on mono PPMs (O on VUs). If another studio is contributing to the programme, the distant operator sends tone to the programme studio where the pre-set level can be adjusted. Once set, the level at the programme studio should have identical readings to that at the distant studio since both will have lined up to the same position on the PPM. The main gain control is also lined up on standard tone, the exact procedure varies from station to station.

Studio preparation
Studio microphones are generally considered as fixtures but even so they do get disconnected and moved around, especially at stations with limited resources, and should be checked before transmission. When extra microphones are being used cables should be lined up neatly to prevent accidents, this also allows much easier tracing if there is a fault. Green and red transmission lights should be working normally before embarking on any major programme. Talkback and cue are also checked because presenters and performers prefer differing headphone levels. Taking level has already been described (see p. 24). During rehearsal the presenter checks through scripts and cues, and if necessary makes notes or marks the scripts.

Recording
If the studio is to feed the master control room or is to be used for recording, a short period of tone is switched through the board. This allows the master control to line up. The tone is left on the tape so that when replaying a programme the tape pre-set is adjusted until a reading of 4 is obtained on the PPM. Further adjustment during transmission should be unnecessary because readings should be similar to those during the recording. Whenever possible during a recording session the programme is monitored from the tape rather than mixer so that any fault in the recording chain is noticed straight away. Unfortunately, this is impossible when an interviewer is making a recording himself because a delay of only a fraction of a second upsets most people's speech when they hear themselves coming back on headphones.

Timing
A stopwatch is essential for recording programmes. If a recording is stopped mid-way or a piece is retaken, the watch is stopped and then restarted when the same point is reached on the retake.

134

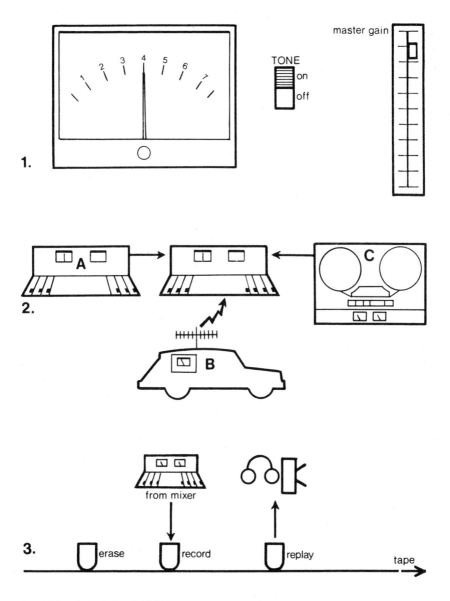

RECORDING AND REHEARSAL

1. Mixers are lined up using a standard tone. Level controls are adjusted so that tone reads 4 on a mono PPM. 2. Various sources may be lined up on tone. A, other studios; B, radio car; C, tapes (with pre-recorded tone at the beginning). 3. A recording may be monitored during programme production. Recording faults become apparent immediately rather than on later playback. The reading is heard a fraction of a second later as it passes over the record head and may be monitored using the pre-fade key on the mixer or direct from the machine, with either headphones or loudspeaker unit. In self-operational situations, it is usually only possible to check the recording periodically because of the upsetting effect a delay can have on speech and timing mixes.

135

Recording Tape

Tape is rather similar to film in a camera. It has a plastic base with an emulsion covering on one side. The most commonly used base is a polyester, an extremely durable material which will not deteriorate under normal conditions. It is so strong that under extreme strain it stretches to hair thickness rather than snap. The emulsion consists of a fine layer of metallic oxide particles bound to the base. During recording, these particles are reorganized into patterns by a magnetic field set up in the recording head. Ferric oxide was widely used until recent years but chromium compounds are now favoured because they give a better signal to noise ratio and wider dynamic range.

Standardization

Tape recorders have to be adjusted to suit the particular kind and brand of tape used so most stations tend to standardize. Tape is made in various thicknesses: the thinner the tape, the longer the recording time available on one reel. Quarter inch wide standard play tape is used in local radio and bought in three reel sizes (the diameter): 5 inches for portable recorders, 7 inches for half-hour programmes, and 10½ inches reels for long recording sessions and hour long programmes. These durations are based on a common speed of 7½ ips though some studios do record musical items at 15 ips to improve quality. Obviously, when you double the speed, you also double the cost of the tape required. The thinner brands of tape are difficult to edit—and in many cases less durable; though long play tape is commonly used and gives better contact with the tape heads.

Reclamation

The advantage of tape over records is that, within reason, it can be reused over and over again. Once a recording is no longer needed, it can be reclaimed. Spare lengths of tape are spliced together to form a complete reel, the original splices checked and remade if necessary. The tape is then bulk erased ready for reissue. Reclaimed tape is quite suitable for recording speech on full-track machines. Different types and thicknesses of tape should never be mixed on one reel. Quality changes can be quite noticeable when listening to a recording made over several different types of tape. Always use the tape the recorder has been adjusted for.

Bulk erasing

Tapes can be completely wiped clean of a recording by using a bulk eraser. On most erasers the tape has to be evenly turned and gently lifted on and off to avoid uneven patterns on the tape. Bulk erasers have a strong magnetic field so watches are removed before using them. A badly erased tape creates a spasmodic hissing effect or allows a previous recording to be heard everytime the tape from a particular section of the reel passes the playback head.

136

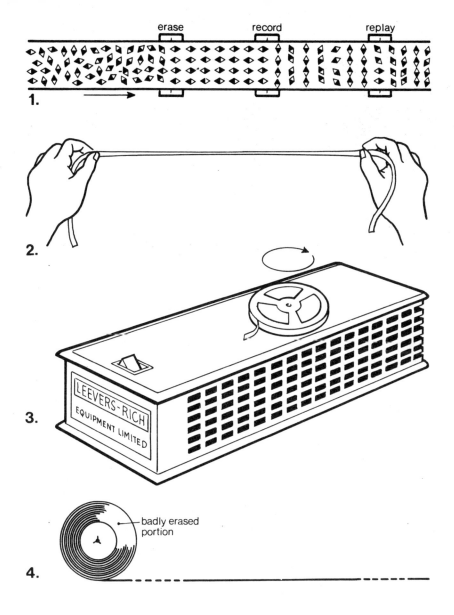

RECORDING TAPE

1. Magnetic particles in unrecorded tape are disaligned. The erase head aligns them and the record head re-arranges them into magnetic patterns, which are invisible, during recording. Tape particles are much more numerous and smaller. 2. Polyester tape stretches under extreme tension to give a bootlace effect. 3. Bulk erasing tape. The reel of tape is turned gently in one direction then the other. Some erasers need only be switched on to adequately erase all the tape.

Tape Care

As with discs, tapes will deteriorate when subjected to dirt, strain and extremes of temperature.

Storage
Tapes are best wrapped in polythene bags and stored in cardboard boxes. Each reel should be labelled to correspond with the notes on the edge of the box. A copy of the cue sheet is also filed with the tape. Boxes are stacked upright because their weight can cause edge crushing or warping in the lower reels of tape, especially if they are unevenly wound on plastic reels. The air conditioning at most local radio stations is quite adequate for tape storage.

Winding
Most reels are double flanged to protect the tape but are usually very flexible at the edges. Tape has to be wound on evenly to prevent the edges being crushed. Very uneven winding can cause the tape edges to warp when stored for long periods. This also occurs if there is a slight bulge as the tape is being wound on. Instead of having a circular shape, the tape takes on an irregular outline. The tension is also important : if it is too slack the layers will rub together when replayed, and may even cause the machine to 'snatch' at the tape; if it is too tight the tape may stretch. Tapes which are stored for long periods should be rewound periodically to prevent print through.

Cleaning
Tape consists of an oxide coating which tends to wear off in minute amounts every time it is played. Oxide particles become deposited on spindles, guides, heads and capstan. A build up of oxide affects the tape transport system and recording and reproducing efficiency. Regular cleaning with a soft rag soaked in methylated spirits is needed.

Magnetization
Tapes are affected by magnetic fields. As well as being cleaned regularly, the tape recorder is also demagnetized. Residual magnetism builds up each time a machine is used for recording purposes. The magnetism consequently affects any recording played on the machine by reducing the high frequency response and increasing noise. Small demagnetizing (degaussing) tools are available for the purpose. Loudspeakers and certain microphones and transformers also affect tapes if too near, even a telephone can cause problems.

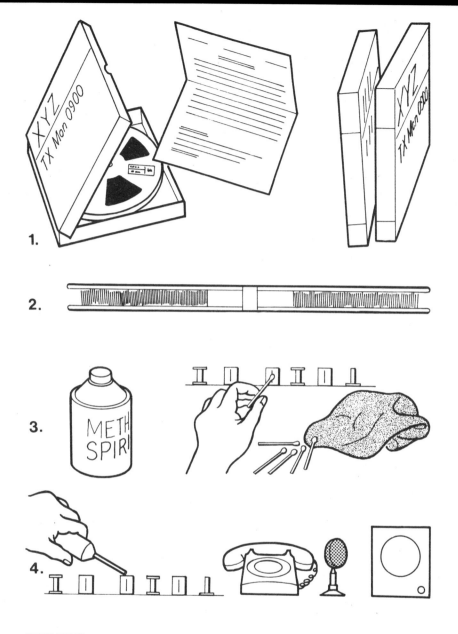

TAPE CARE
1. Tapes are stored in boxes and labelled along the spine. The reel is also labelled to correspond with the spine, and a cue sheet enclosed. 2. Uneven winding can damage the tape edges, especially if reels are incorrectly stored e.g. one on top of another. 3. Tape transport mechanisms and tape heads are cleaned with soft cloths and cotton buds soaked in methylated spirits (methanol). 4. Heads and guides may be demagnetized to remove residual magnetism which affects tapes. Keep tapes away from telephones, microphones and transformers, and loudspeakers.

Recording and Replay Faults

These can be divided into three categories:
1. Faulty recording equipment causing poor recordings,
2. Bad operational technique providing poor signal during recording,
3. Faulty tape.

Equipment

Tape heads have to be cleaned regularly to obtain a good, smooth contact with the tape, without any gaps.

Professional machines hold the tape against the heads by tension, but on home and several semiprofessional machines pressure pads are used. These are also checked to see they provide enough pressure. Poor tape/head contact leads to loss of the higher frequencies on record and playback.

Tape speed is also affected on portable tape recorders run off batteries. As the batteries lose power beyond a lower limit the tape speed starts to drop. Consequently when a tape recorded on such a machine is replayed on a studio tape recorder the sound seems to get progressively faster. To a certain extent recordings made at the wrong speed can be salvaged by replaying the tape with the tape recorder speed adjusted to match the recording. This is then copied off onto a studio machine running at the correct speed.

When two recordings are heard together on a full-track machine it is usually because the tape has been recorded on a half-track machine, with both tracks used. Very rarely does this mean the tape recorder erase head is faulty (therefore not wiping off the previous recording.)

Operations

Noise is present throughout the broadcasting chain. For all practical purposes, the programme is sent along the chain at the highest levels possible without distorting. If the levels are too low, therefore, the noise becomes more noticeable, and if too high causes distortion. The tape has to be correctly modulated: under-modulation causes hiss; over-modulation causes distortion.

Tape

There are numerous kinds of tape faults (see p. 150).

COMMON RECORDING AND REPRODUCTION FAULTS

Dirty heads e.g. covered in wax pencil marks.

Overmodulated and undermodulation.

Twist in tape.

Half-track recording replayed on a full-track machine.

Bad edits and dirt on tape.

Patches of tape particles missing.

Incorrect storage—magnets (in loudspeakers etc.) excessive heat and humidity affect tape.

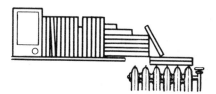

Flat batteries (in portable tape recorders).

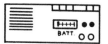

Incompletely (bulk) erased tape.

Tracks

Local radio uses quarter inch wide tape on full- or half-track (or 2 track) tape recorders.

Full-track machines
These are used in monophonic broadcasting and record over the whole width of the tape.

Half-track mono
These record over the top part of the tape, therefore offering two tracks. The second track is used by turning the tape over on to the other edge. Most portable reel-to-reel machines are half-track recorders. Bulk-erased tape has to be used on these machines when the recording is to be played back on a full-track machine (which replays both tracks simultaneously). The second track is rarely used because it prevents tapes being played on full-track machines. It cannot be edited either, because a cut on one track would spoil the other.

   Full-track recordings, however, can easily be played on half-track machines, though only half the recorded area is reproduced.

Half-track stereo
Stereo heads are able to work on top and bottom tracks simultaneously. Half-track mono recordings can also be made or played back on a stereo machine by using only the upper track. As on mono half-track machines, full-track recordings may be played back on a stereo recorder.

   Stereo half-track recordings for mono reproduction are best mixed down to one channel rather than played on a full-track machine to combine the tracks.

Levels
Recordings made on full and half tracks cannot easily be edited together because of a noticeable difference in level. The easiest and most reliable way is to dub the whole programme or inserts onto another machine rather than edit different track configurations together.

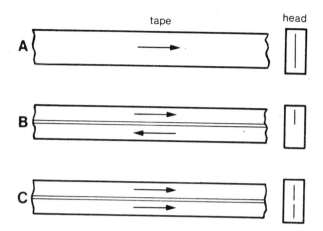

tape head

TAPE TRACKS

A, Full-track recordings occupy the full width of the tape; B, half-track recordings occupy almost half the width of the tape. On mono recorders, the top track only is used. When tape is turned over the other edge may be utilized thus giving two tracks—running in opposite directions. C, half-track stereo recorders use the two edges of tape simultaneously. The left channel is recorded on the top track, and the right channel on the bottom.

Dubbing

Tapes are copied to:
1. Control levels and introduce extra effects e.g. fades, 2. Improve the quality e.g. to remove hiss using a filter.
3. Change speed or tracks to standardize the tape for transmission or to make tape editing easier by copying at a higher speed.
4. Transfer to a different system e.g. reel to cartridge, or cassette to reel.

Copying
Tapes are re-recorded to give similar levels to the originals (unless they have been incorrectly recorded). If the tape to be copied has tone at the beginning this is simply lined up to read 4 on the PPM, otherwise the pre-set is adjusted to give reasonable readings throughout the tape, just as in the line up procedure for transmitting or mixing a programme. If the tape is being dubbed to control levels then obviously these must be monitored as the tape is being recorded.

Standardization
Studio tape machines at each station are standardized in speed and number of tracks so that a recording made on one may be reproduced on another. Problems arise when tapes have been recorded on other machines with different running speeds or tracks. For convenience, non-standard recordings are copied onto studio tape recorders. The slower running speed of cassettes, for example, makes it difficult to cue up or edit recordings, so they are copied onto quarter inch tape before broadcasting. Stations which use only full-track (monophonic) machines also have to dub half-track recordings to full-track if both tracks have been used. Cartridge machines are now almost exclusively employed at many stations for tape inserts so items have to be copied from reel-to-reel machines onto cartridges.

High-speed copying
Time can be saved when copying from reel to reel by replaying and recording at higher speeds e.g. if the tape to be copied has been recorded at 7½ ips it can be replayed at 15 ips and a copy taken on a second machine also running at 15 ips. When the copy is played back at 7½ ips it sounds at the normal speed. Almost any speed can be used in dubbing providing replay and record machines run at the same speed. A similar system is used to obtain copies at lower speeds e.g. 7½ ips to 3¾ ips. The tape to be copied is simply played at twice its normal speed and re-recorded onto a machine set to the normal speed. The copy will thus sound twice its normal speed in effect halving the replay speed of the tape. High-speed copying causes loss of high frequencies and owing to slight speed variations will cause differences in programme duration.

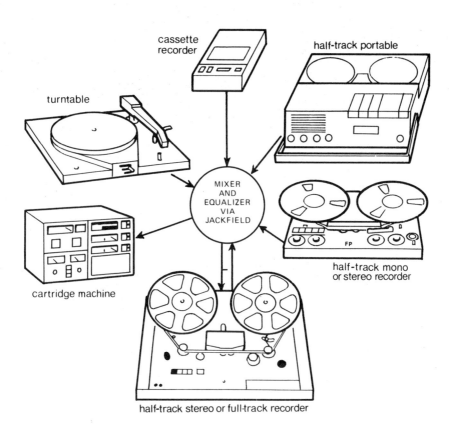

cassette recorder

half-track portable

turntable

MIXER AND EQUALIZER VIA JACKFIELD

half-track mono or stereo recorder

cartridge machine

half-track stereo or full-track recorder

Master recorded at ips	Replay master at ips	Record copy at ips	Playback speed ips	Advantage
$7\frac{1}{2}$	15	15	$7\frac{1}{2}$	Dubbing at higher speed saves time
$7\frac{1}{2}$	15	$7\frac{1}{2}$	$3\frac{3}{4}$	Dubbing down at high speed saves time
$7\frac{1}{2}$	$7\frac{1}{2}$	15	15	Dubbing up to 15 ips makes editing easier

DUBBINGS
Dubbing facilities allow material from almost any source to be copied on to cartridge or reel-to-reel machines for reproduction on standard studio tape machines. Dubbing allows special treatment e.g. adjusting the speed of a recording made on a portable tape recorder with flat batteries; removing tape hiss, etc.

145

Splicing

Tape recorders used for editing are fitted with an aluminium cutting block, this has an open channel for gripping the tape, and two cutting grooves for guiding the razor blade. One groove is at right angles to the groove and normally only used for repairing tape, and the other at 45°. Angled cuts are used so that the sound fades in or out at the splice therefore creating a slight overlap or an easing in rather than a sudden changeover.

Tape is smoothed down in the channel with the emulsion side face down. Cutting marks (see p. 148) are positioned along the 45° groove and a single edged razor blade drawn across the tape or mechanical scissors used. Unwanted sections are removed; the two ends are pushed together in the channel so that their 45° cuts match and just touch without overlap or gap. After removing the wax pencil marks, the ends are joined with splicing tape. Approximately one inch of splicing tape is placed neatly over the tape so that the adhesive edges do not overlap. Once the sticky tape has been positioned it is gently rubbed down with the fingers to remove air patches. Splicing tape is narrower than quarter inch magnetic tape so it does not have to be trimmed along the edges after editing.

The tape is removed from the channel by gently lifting it upwards at an angle—not straight up because it can cause the tape edges to distort.

Leader

Coloured non-magnetic tape is attached to recording tape to mark the beginning and end, and sometimes to signify the kind of recording, e.g. white-blue flashed leader can mean 7½ ips stereo, white-red 15 ips stereo, with pure red for 15 ips mono and pure blue for 7½ ips mono. The practice varies from station to station but originally white was used to mark the beginning of mono tapes, yellow between multibanded inserts, and red for the end. Leader is attached to tapes at the beginning of modulation—the point at which its transmission is to begin. Leader is not used to insert pauses or lengthen items because sudden lack of background noise (due to absence of a recorded signal) is quite noticeable.

SPLICING

Aluminium splicing blocks have a channel for gripping the tape, and two cutting grooves 45° and 90°.

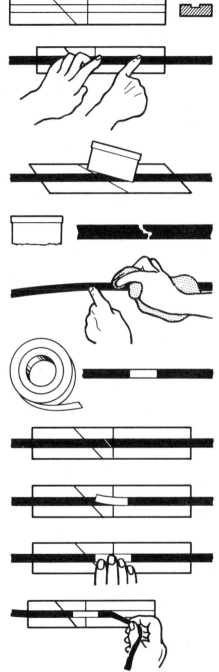

The tape is smoothed emulsion side down in the channel.

Cutting marks are positioned over the 45° groove and a single edged razor blade drawn across at angles or approximately 30°.

Worn blades cause jagged cuts and damage cutting grooves.

Wax pencil marks are removed before splicing.

Professional splicing tape is fractionally narrower than magnetic tape.

Tapes to be joined are butted together without overlap or gap.

A short piece of splicing tape is placed on top (laying down one end first to avoid creases and air bubbles).

The splice is gently rubbed over to ensure good contact.

Tape is removed by pulling gently sideways.

147

Editing Techniques

Editing may be required to:
1. Reduce the duration of a programme or item.
2. Structure the programme to give a decided order.
3. Remove retakes, fluffs, and other faults.
4. Prepare the tape for transmission e.g. banding, attaching leader etc.

Where to cut
The tape is listened to first before deciding on any cuts. If pieces are to be removed, the tape is rewound and the first unwanted section found. The controls vary from machine to machine but on most a pause control allows the tape to remain in contact with the heads whilst reeling by hand. With experience individual words and letters can be recognized when the tape is moved slowly by hand. A mark is made with a yellow wax pencil on the tape just before the beginning of the unwanted piece yet leaving the space or breath pause between words. The tape is then reeled on by hand to the end of the unwanted piece and a similar mark made just before the first word of the wanted section. The marks must be as close as possible without cutting into words. The tape is then pulled away from the heads and cuts made at the two points using a splicing block (see p. 146), the unwanted piece removed and the tape rejoined. Usually, it is better to leave the pause in before the first cut than use the one at the second cut because the beginning of a new word comes in more cleanly than the end, thus masking a splice more effectively. Edits are far more noticeable when made in the middle of a pause between words.

Rough editing
When producing a feature, for example, items may have been recorded in a different order to the one required for the programme. This can be corrected by dubbing off (see p. 146) items in the correct order or cut out the pieces and put them on separate spools. Short lengths can be strung out along a table top. It helps to write a brief headline on the tape to show which piece is which and also to indicate which is the beginning.

Fine editing
Parts of words may be removed, pauses added, and speech condensed by careful editing. The golden rule at this stage of editing though is: *if in doubt—leave it!* Good editing should not be noticed. A bad edit can destroy good work by drawing attention to faults. Explosive sounds like bs and ps as well as the letters d, k and t are relatively easy to locate in editing but only by listening can an editor decide whether or not an edit will work. Sometimes a slightly longer pause can be cut in to mask any change in speech pattern when a sentence or two has been cut out. Atmosphere from the original recording is used for this purpose—*not yellow leader tape.*

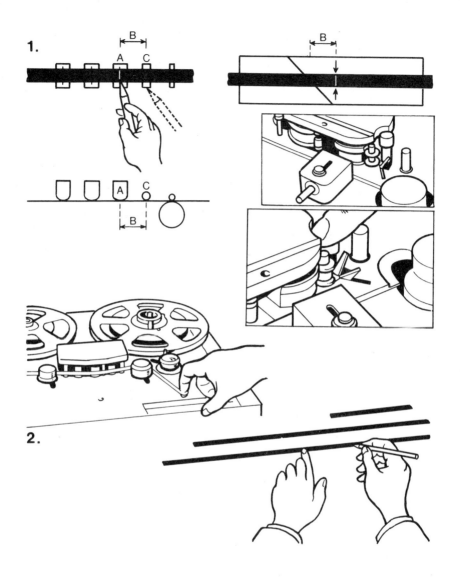

EDITING TECHNIQUES

1. A wax pencil is used to mark cutting points on the tape over either the replay head (A) or a predetermined position (B), also marked out on the editing block, away from the head, e.g. a tape guide (C). 2. Some machines have edit or pause controls which allow the tape to be manipulated without any tension or drive applied by the motors. Tape can therefore be easily pulled away from the heads for editing on the tape deck. During editing items may be kept on separate reels or, in the case of short lengths of tape, placed in rows on a table top.

Faulty Splices

Faulty splices using adhesive tape are often noticeable and can even lead to programme breakdowns or tape machine faults. Some of the common mistakes and their effects are:

1. Too much adhesive tape. This reduces the flexibility of the tape leading to poor contact with the playback head.

2. Too little adhesive tape. Splice may break.

3. Misalignment. Causes azimuth error as tape passes the playback head. Particularly noticeable on half-track and stereo recordings.

4. Protruding adhesive tape (often caused by 3). This sticks to the tape guides and heads causing jolts. A very sticky tape may even cause a machine to stop or start wrapping round the capstan.

5. Moisture or grease on the adhesive or recording tape. The splice may not hold together. Avoid handling the tapes.

6. Overlapping joint. This causes drop out as one section is momentarily lifted away from the playback head.

7. Gap between recording tape at splice. Causes drop out. Bare adhesive tape also sticks to guides etc.

8. Jagged ends at the joint. These are caused by cutting with a blunt razor blade, and lead to drop out because of either missing tape particles in a gap or an overlap.

9. Wavy edges (edge stretch) near the splice. These are caused by suddenly pulling the tape from the editing block. Effect is variable depending on degree of stretching.

10. Air bubbles and dirt. Always clean off any marks before splicing tapes together and smooth out the adhesive tape.

Recording

If a recording is being made on a reel of tape containing splices, it should be checked first to see they are properly made. A recording made over a poor edit cannot be improved by remaking the splice.

COMMON FAULTS

Splicing tape too long.

Splicing tape too short.

Tape incorrectly lined up.

Protruding adhesive tape.

Greasy splicing tape peels off.

Tape overlap.

Tape gap.

Torn ends, caused by worn razor blade.

Wavy edge—stress distortion.

Air bubbles and dirt trapped under splice.

151

Echo

Large broadcasting organizations have echo chambers. These are rooms with sound reflecting walls (rather like a bathroom) containing a loudspeaker and a microphone for picking up the reverberation. A clean feed i.e. without echo of the mixer output or a particular source is taken to the loudspeaker and the resulting echo picked up by the microphone and mixed into the programme.

Reverberation plate and spring
Although reverberation plates work in two directions only, the resulting sound is hard to distinguish from echo chambers. They consist of a transducer (which turn electrical signals into vibrations) attached to one end of a metal plate, and a pick-up transducer, which acts as a microphone, attached to the other end. The source from the mixer is fed to the transmitter transducer which produces vibrations throughout the metal sheet. These are then picked up by the other transducer, and the resulting reverberation fed back for mixing into the programme. A cheaper system which relies on similar action employs a spring suspended between transducers. Unfortunately spring systems produce a more mechanical sound.

Tape feedback
An echo sound can be created by tape recording the original sound and replaying it a fraction of a second later. A way of doing this is to re-record the item with the replaying fader open and the recording fader slightly open on the mixer. The signal into the tape machine is recorded and replayed momentarily later as it passes over the playback head. This signal is then fed back to the mixer. A more refined way is to use a tape loop or drum passing over a combination of playback heads in a row after the record head. Feedback echo sounds more mechanical than that from reverberation plates, and sounds better at faster speeds.

Uses
Music which has been recorded in a room with relatively dead acoustics can be enlivened by the addition of artificial reverberation. As well as its obvious use in drama, echo is also used in advertisements and promotions (trailers) to reinforce voices or for musical effects.

Music
Musical endings to trailers should have a fade or decay. If the music has had to be shortened a small amount of echo at the end helps to restore the effect of reverberation which would normally be heard (and which is lost through editing).

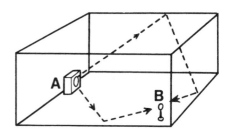

Echo chamber Room with sound reflecting walls. Sound from a loudspeaker (A) is reflected and picked up by a microphone (B).

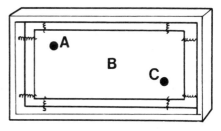

Reverberation Plate
A drive unit (A) induces sound waves into the metal plate (B) suspended in a frame. A contract microphone (C) picks up the vibrations.

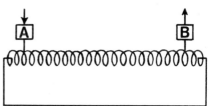

Spring
A transducer (A) creates vibrations, which are picked up at the other end of the spring by another transducer (B).

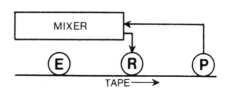

Feedback
A feed of the replay head can be remixed back into a programme during a recording.

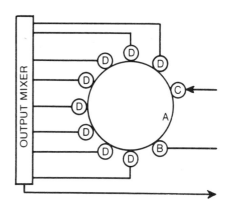

Magnetic loop or drum
A drum or continuous loop (A) of magnetic tape is driven continuously so that first of all it is demagnetized by the erase head (B). The input is then recorded (C) and replayed successively by a series of replay heads (D) linked to a small mixing unit.

153

Modern Technology

New equipment and methods of broadcasting are continually being developed thus offering an improved and varied kind of service to the listener. Two notable advances in broadcasting technology affecting local radio are the Dolby noise reduction systems and traffic news signalling.

Dolby noise reduction system
Many of the operations in a broadcasting chain can introduce noise. This is particularly so when tape recording and in the stereo transmission of programmes (there being far more background noise on a stereo programme compared with a programme received in mono from the same transmitter). The signal to noise ratio can be improved by companding—a process involving the compression of the programme before recording and expansion (the opposite effect) on playback. The problems are making the expansion exactly match the compression over the whole frequency and dynamic ranges, and preventing background noise going up and down with the signal.

A method of overcoming these problems has been developed by Dolby. There are two systems: Dolby A, a complex system used in professional recording studios; and Dolby B, a less complicated system used on items to be heard domestically e.g. records and FM broadcasting.

Traffic information
There are three main ways of giving traffic information over the air:
1. On a national station—in which case traffic announcements for the whole country are given out.
2. From a network of transmitters using a single frequency specially allocated to just motoring information with only the transmitters in the area of each message being switched on.
3. On local or regional stations between or during programmes (the system used in West Germany, Austria and Switzerland).

Obviously the latter two methods are to be preferred because of their involvement with only local motoring information. Signals are incorporated with each bulletin causing car radios which have been specially built for this purpose to automatically tune over. This allows a driver to listen to cassettes/cartridges, or a particular station yet still receive any essential motoring news for his area. The car radio may also be switched to receive only traffic news—with silence between the messages.

154

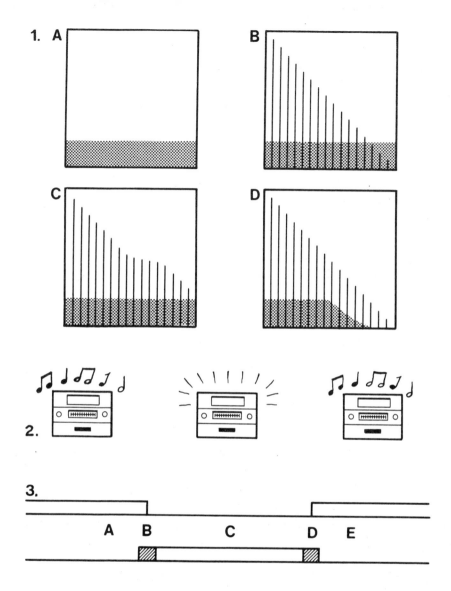

MODERN TECHNOLOGY

1. The Dolby System. A, noise is present on all tape recordings and on FM stereo reception. B, although most of the programme or music masks the noise it is possible for low level sounds to be lost in the noise. C, in a Dolby system the parts likely to be lost in noise are increased in level—the system being able to distinguish different frequencies and levels. D, on playback or reception a Dolby circuit is used to reduce the level of all the parts which were increased, leaving the lower levels more free of noise.

2. Operating sequence of a car radio for automatic switching to traffic news. A, another station or cassette etc. B, start signal causes automatic switching of the car radio. C, traffic announcement. D, finish signal allows car radio to switch back. E, cassette player output or other radio station.

Further Reading

BARON, MIKE,
Independent Radio. Terence Dalton, Lavenham, Suffolk (1975).
The story of commercial radio in the United Kingdom.

BBC HANDBOOK,
BBC Publications, London.
Includes details about BBC local radio stations, produced annually.

IBA HANDBOOK,
IBA London.
A guide to independent broadcasting in the United Kingdom including the
ILR stations, produced annually.

IBA TECHNICAL REVIEW N'2—TECHNICAL REFERENCE BOOK,
IBA, London (revised edition 1974).
Includes code of practice for independent local radio studio performance.

IBA TECHNICAL REVIEW N'5—INDEPENDENT LOCAL RADIO,
IBA, London (1974).
Covers engineering planning, the equipment at transmitting stations and
control equipment. Also includes a section on the design and operation of a
studio centre for independent local radio.

JOHNSON, JOSEPH S. and JONES, KENNETH K.,
Modern Radio Station Practices. Wadsworth, Belmont, California, (1972)
and Prentice Hall, Hemel Hempstead.
American methods including details of commercial aspects of broadcasting
and sales.

MILLER, G. M. (editor),
BBC Pronouncing Dictionary of British Names. Oxford University Press,
London (1971).
This is the most popular of all British pronouncing dictionaries and used by
studios all over the world. It is based on more than forty years of research by
the BBC into pronounciation of British place names and personal names.

NISBETT, ALEC,
The Technique of the Sound Studio. Focal Press, London, and Focal/
Hastings House, New York (3rd edn, 1972).
A comprehensive examination of programme operations in studios large
and small including stereo techniques.

NISBETT, ALEC,
The Use of Microphones. Focal Press, London, and Focal/Hastings House,
New York (1975).
A detailed study of the range and use of broadcast microphones, with
emphasis on position, balance and control of them.

Glossary

Actuality (80, 81) Sound recorded at an event as distinct from effects on disc etc., used to illustrate items.

Adaptors (41) Convert tape decks for use with different reels, e.g. cine reels to NAB reels.

Agency (10) News agency supplying material in written form via a tele-printer or verbally via telephone. They may also offer tape recorded interviews to stations either directly or by line.

Apparatus room/bays (14, 16) Area where incoming and outgoing lines are terminated along with ancillary equipment e.g. jackfields, power units, amplifiers and equalizers etc.

Attenuation (14, 15) Reduction in level of programme signal.

Audition key (22, 24) Pre-fade key or switch used for monitoring a source without fading it up (US).

Back announcement (78) Reference to an item or programme just heard.

Backing track Background music a disc jockey uses when making long announcements. A DJ may have his own regular backing tracks recorded on cartridges.

Balance (26) The positioning of microphones to obtain a good signal, discriminate against noise, and provide a high ratio of direct sound to indirect sound.

Bands (42, 43) Sections of tape separated by leader on one reel. In the same way, different sections or tracks on a record are referred to as bands.

Bar Graph Meter (32, 33) Measures programme volume, displaying level as a strip of light which lengthens or shortens within a fixed scale.

Bidirectional microphone (86–88, 90, 91) Microphone which picks up sound mainly to the front and rear and is almost dead at the sides. This gives a figure of eight response.

Board (18) Control panel (US).

Break (62, 63) Pause in a programme or between programmes for com-mercials, news etc., hence 'newsbreak', 'commercial break' and so.

Broadcast chain (10) Course a signal takes from studio to transmitter.

Bulk erasing (136, 137) The complete erasure of signals recorded on a reel of tape or cartridge in one operation.

Cans Broadcasting expression for headphones.

Capstan (38, 39) Drive spindle on tape deck.

Cardioid microphone (86–88) Microphone with heart-shaped response.

Cartridge (44, 45) Plastic case holding endless loop of ¼ inch wide tape wound on a revolving core used for short news inserts, jingles, commer-cials etc. Tape moves in one direction only.

Cassette (98, 99) Not to be confused with cartridges these use narrower tape and may be wound end to end. In UK only occasionally used for interviews—recordings have to be dubbed onto ¼ inch tape for editing.

Channel (22) Fader, preset/coarse gain control, and pan pot etc., associated with each source routed through the mixer. These facilities may be built into a single module for each channel.

Censor key/button (120) Switch for cutting a source or programme off the air e.g. during a phone-in using a tape delay when profanity occurs. The delay allows the presenter time to react and press the button.

Clean feed (118) A feed of programme back to an outside source e.g. remote studio (using a control line) or telephone caller, without the contribution from that source.

Clock (74, 75) Diagram showing a presenter or DJ the format or sequence of items and records within an hour or set period of a programme. Also called a wheel.

Coarse gain control (22, 23) Used before faders for roughly pre-setting levels of sources before being faded up.

Compressor (18, 19) Automatically reduces the dynamic range of a signal. Different degrees of compression can be selected.

Condenser microphone (86, 87) Uses varying capacitance between two charged plates—a fixed base plate and a diaphragm (or one diaphragm and another)—to create an electrical signal. When the diaphragm vibrates minute changes in distance occur between that and the base plate thus varying the capacitance.

Continuity (62) Links between programmes which may include introductions, back announcements (credits etc.), trailers, announcements, and station identification (idents).

Contribution circuit (132) Line for sending programme items from station to station.

Control board (18) Control desk or panel (US).

Control desk (16, 18) A construction holding the mixer, control panel, switches, headphone sockets, and associated equipment for programme and station operations.

Control line (11, 14, 15) Circuit between one studio or outside source, and another for talkback and cueing purposes. Usually telephone circuits though higher quality music lines may be used.

Control room (16, 17) The production and operational area associated with a studio, containing turntables, tape machines, control board etc. Since programmes are mixed and monitored here, the room is usually acoustically treated in the same way as a studio.

Cross-fade (84, 85) A mix from one source to another, fading one out as the other is being faded in.

Cross-plugging (84, 85) Plugging from one jack (or socket) to another usually on the jackfield or patch panel.

Cross-talk (42) Interference (induction) from one circuit leaking into another.

Cue (36, 37) An indication usually to start a particular operation or announcement. Cues may be written (in the form of a cue sheet), verbal (on talkback or on air), or visual (hand or light cues).

Cue light (36, 37) Lamp signal to start. Occasionally used for other signalling e.g. slow down, speed up etc., when used in pre-arranged way.

Cue material (78, 79, 130, 132) Material given to the presenter for introducing and back-announcing an item or programme.

158

Cue programme (11, 15) A feed of programme for cueing. Often associated with the talkback circuit. In the normal position cue programme is extended and when the switch is pressed talkback is put onto the circuit.

Cue sheet (78, 79) Script with programme (or insert) introduction and back-announcement. Other details are usually given including date, duration, and transmission time etc.

Cut (42) A tape insert separated by leader tape from others on a multi-banded reel. Sometimes also used to describe the different tracks or bands on an long playing record.

Decibel, dB (32) A measure of the volume of sound—a unit used for comparing levels of sound intensity. Differences in intensity are calculated as $10 \log_{10} (I^2/I^1)$ where I^2 and I^1 are the different intensities, e.g. a rise of 10 dB indicates a tenfold increase in intensity.

Degauss (138) Demagnetize.

DIN (40) Deutsche Industrie Norm—a German standards system. DIN type sideless reels are used in Europe. DIN adaptors are available on some tape machines for converting to or from cine and NAB reels.

Distribution system (130, 131) A line from a central source for supplying several stations simultaneously with programmes and programme material. News may be sent this way at regular intervals by a national newsroom or agency.

Dolby (154, 155) Noise reduction system in recording and transmission.

Double ender (20, 21) Cable with plug at each end for making connections between lines and equipment on the jackfield.

Double take (122) A repetition of an operation, word, sentence or item incorrectly presented during a recording.

Drop out (150) Loss of signal in a tape recording caused by faults in the magnetic emulsion or faulty splices.

Dubbing (144, 145) Copying.

Dynamic microphone (86, 87) Uses a small moving coil suspended in the field of a permanent magnet. Movement generates a current in the coil. The term 'moving coil' microphone is more precise.

Dynamic range (28) The range of sound levels the transmission chain can take without noticeable noise at the lower levels and distortion at higher levels.

Echo (152, 153) Repetition of a sound by reflection. The continued reflection of a sound, from wall to wall for example, is called reverberation though the word 'echo' is now often used (incorrectly).

Edging in (84, 85) A fading in technique used where inserts would normally come in with too much force on a fully opened fader. The insert is introduced at a slightly lower level and then quickly brought up to the correct level. This is also useful when dealing, at short notice, with live inserts of unknown volume.

Editing (146–149) The addition, removal and re-assembly of tape recorded material usually carried out by cutting the tape with a blade and sticking it together with special adhesive tape.

Effects microphone (112, 113) Used at sports stadia and other outside broadcasts for achieving the correct blend of background sound when using a lip microphone for commentary.

Equalizer (14, 15) Apparatus for compensating for attenuation distortion in lines.

Fader (22, 23) Device for fading sources in or out.

Feedback (12, 13) The build-up of sound to a howl caused when a microphone picks up its own amplified output from a loudspeaker. Also known as howlround.

Fluff (122, 123) A word or line incorrectly spoken.

FM, frequency modulation (48) A method of transmitting the programme by changing the *frequency* of the carrier wave in proportion to the amplitude of the programme signal.

Frequency response (14, 34) The level at which different frequencies may be held in relation to each other when passing through equipment etc., e.g. microphone, lines etc.

Gain (22–25) Amplification.

Hard wired (20) Permanently wired.

Heads (38, 39) Erase, record and replay heads of a tape recorder.

Hiss (34) High frequency noise.

In cue (78, 79) The first few words or details of how a tape starts.

Insert (42, 43, 88, 118) Live or recorded items placed in a programme. They may be on tape, telephone line, from the radio car, remote source (sports stadia for example), or simply live from a studio.

ips (38) Inches per second.

Jackfield (20, 21) A multiple row of jack sockets used for overplugging and connecting equipment and lines. All studio and control room equipment is wired via the jackfield to enable faulty apparatus to be replaced in a circuit without affecting the programme. Lines and extra facilities may be connected in a similar way.

Jack plug (20, 21) Usually at each end of a double-ender for making interconnections on the jackfield and connecting extra facilities.

Junction (62, 63) The point where one programme ends and another begins, sometimes with a continuity announcement between them.

Leader (146) Uncoated tape attached to the beginning of a tape for threading and lining up with the heads (the join marking the beginning of the tape). Various colours and markings are now used by stations according to tape speed and whether in mono or stereo. Leader is also used to separate tape inserts when multibanded on a single reel. Traditionally, white was used as a leader and yellow for inserts.

Level (24, 25, 28, 29) The loudness of sound as measured on a meter, i.e. PPM, VU meter or bar graph meter.

Limiter (18, 19, 30, 31) A device which automatically prevents sources or the programme from exceeding a predetermined level.

Lines (18, 19, 30, 31) Wires to and from the radio station for the sending of programme and instructions: music lines are used for programme purposes and control lines for production instructions.

Line-up tone (134) Pure tone, i.e. a single frequency, usually at 1000 Hertz at a fixed level for use in lining up equipment. The tone should read the same level on meters at any stage of the transmission chain. Tone at zero level should reach 4 on a PPM (equivalent to 40% modulation at the transmitter) zero level being one milliwatt in 600 ohms.

Lip microphone (112, 113) A robust kind of ribbon microphone held close to the mouth and used for commentating. Excludes background sound.

Log (58, 59) A record of parts or the whole of the station's output listing items broadcast and faults. Separate logs may be kept for programmes, music, commercials, and faults or operational errors.

Long play tape (136) Thinner tape allowing more (half as much again) to be stored on a reel compared with the standard type. It also gives slightly better contact with heads because of its greater flexibility but is not as robust as standard play tape.

Master Control Room, MCR (52, 53) Main control room usually fitted as a studio or with a studio attached, used both for producing (or replaying) programmes and for switching the output of other studios to the transmitters. It is also the main monitoring area of the station's output and usually associated with apparatus bays.

Microphone cut switch (36, 37) Cuts off the presenter's microphone when held down. Also known as a cough switch and sometimes combined with talkback—routing the microphone from the programme chain to the talkback circuit.

Modulation (32) Alteration of the amplitude of frequency of radio carrier wave by the programme signal, 100% modulation corresponding to maximum level acceptable at the transmitter without causing distortion. The term is also used to describe the signal recorded on a disc.

Monitoring (46, 47, 50, 51) Checking the quality of sources and programmes. Can also mean listening to income sources e.g. network lines, when preparing to join them etc.

Moving coil microphone (86, 87) A more precise term for a dynamic microphone using a small moving coil suspended in the field of a permanent magnet. Movement generates a current in the coil.

Music line (10, 11, 14, 15) A high quality land line used for programme purposes.

NAB spool (40, 41) Usually 10½ in. in diameter with a large centre hub.

Noise (12, 13, 154, 155) Unwanted sound. Several forms: that picked up by the microphone; mechanical noise introduced by equipment e.g. rumble from turntables; and noise introduced by circuits in the broadcast chain.

Omnidirectional microphone (86, 87) Microphone with all round response.

Opting (128) The practice of leaving or joining a network for programmes.

Out cue (78, 79) Details of how a tape ends.

Outside broadcast, OB (14, 15, 100, 101, 106, 107) Live or recorded programme from radio car or truck, live programmes being sent by radio link or line.

Outside source (10, 20) Programme source from outside the studio.

Overplugging (20, 21) Plugging made on a jackfield to bypass circuits or equipment, e.g. when there is a fault, and for connecting extra equipment.

Package (66) Collection of items or inserts presented as a whole.

Pan pot, panoramic potentiometer (22, 23) Used for giving a mono source e.g. studio microphones, a stereo image by increasing the level fed to one side of the mixer's main channels at the expense of the other.

PasB, programme as broadcast (58) Log of programmes and contents.

Patch cord (20) Similar to a double ender for making connections on a patch panel.

Patch panel (16, 17) Equivalent of a jackfield.

Peak programme meter, PPM (32, 33) Used for measuring programme volume. Has a simple scale marked 1 to 7 and linear in decibels over most of it.

Pilot tone system (48) Method of transmitting in stereo.

Pinch wheel (39) Pressure roller holding tape against drive capstan or spindle on a tape deck.

Platter (70) The top rotating plate of a turntable. Also describes records.

Popping (24) The temporary breakup of the signal from a microphone caused by explosive consonants, mainly p and b, when speaking too close to the microphone. A windshield helps reduce this effect.

Pot cut (84, 85) On air editing of a tape insert by swiftly fading it out.

Pre-fade (22, 23, 82, 83) Checking a source for level and quality etc., before fading it up. Also means playing music (signature tunes etc.) at a predetermined point and fading up for the remaining time when leading up to a fixed point e.g. end of programme, newsbreak etc.

Presence (34, 35) The boosting of part of the frequency range to make particular sounds stand out from the rest. In music this can give the effect of picking out particular instruments.

Pre-set gain control (22, 23) Used before faders for roughly setting levels before being faded up. Sometimes called coarse gain control.

Print through (138) The magnetic pattern of one layer of tape re-aligning (re-recording) the next layer in a reel of tape. This gives a faint copy of the original signal. Print through can occur quite naturally when a tape is stored over a long period of time. Tape recordings in store should be re-wound from time to time. Adverse conditions, temperature and shock, can also cause print through.

Private line (14) Control line (US).

Programme A complete production. Also means the signal of a programme in production or being transmitted.

Promotion (64, 65) Live or recorded item advertising programmes.

Rack room (14) Apparatus room (US).

Radio link (104, 105) Radio circuit. An alternative to using a land line for sending programmes back to the studio centre.

Radio car (100–103) Vehicle fitted with simple mixing equipment, two way radio for talkback with the studio, and a high-quality transmitter (connected to an aerial or antenna mounted on a telescopic mast) for programme material. Used extensively for live news and topical inserts.

Radio microphone (104, 105) Microphone with a small transmitter attached. Transmission range is very short. In local radio they can be very useful when reporting away from the radio car—freeing the broadcaster of trailing cables.

Radio telephone (104, 105) Two-way radio either for direct communication with the studio or through the public telephone system.

Relay service (10) Programmes sent by land line to listeners' homes. Relay companies usually offer their subscribers a wide range of radio and television stations by line, sometimes including their own community TV programmes.

Remote (100) Outside broadcast (US).

Remote studio (108, 109) Small studio in another area away from the main station connected by line.

Response shaping (34) Adjusting particular narrow bands of frequencies using filters and amplifiers.

Reverberation (152) Reflection of sound from surface to surface, the word echo commonly being used (incorrectly) to describe this effect.

Reverse talkback (17, 36) Talkback from the studio to the control room.

Ribbon microphone (86, 87) Bidirectional microphone which uses a narrow strip of foil supported within a strong magnetic field.

Ring main (46) Rotary (multiway) switch used for selecting sources and programmes for monitoring. Sometimes also used to describe the multiway switches for selecting sources on mixer faders.

ROT, recording off transmission (46) Recording made from a station's transmission. The term usually means recording a station's output rather than actually recording reception from the transmitters, when a copy of a live programme (for repeating later) is needed.

Running order (77, 126) List of items within a programme, giving titles and duration.

Segue (84, 85) Musical or speech insert immediately following another. A record may thus follow straight on from a recorded interview.

Sequence programme (74) Programme with a planned structure often called a strip programme.

Shellac (72) Material from which early records (78 rpm) were made. Soluble in methylated spirits.

Signal (50) Electrical or electromagnetic transmission carrying programme.

Signal to noise ratio (153) Ratio of programme sound to unwanted sound i.e. noise.

Simultaneous broadcast, sb (128) A programme or item broadcast by two or more stations at the same time.

Slip mat (70, 71) Loose or fixed felt mat used for slipping records on a moving turntable during lining up.

Speaker (90) Person speaking into microphone. Can also mean loudspeaker.

Splicing (146) Joining two pieces of tape.

Station identification (ident) (62) Name of the station, often with the frequency, given live or in the form of a jingle.

Stroboscope (70) Used for checking speed of equipment. Basically consists of a light source at a particular fixed frequency and markings or holes on the main moving part of the equipment e.g. edge of turntable. When the equipment is moving at correct constant speed the markings appear stationary viewed in this light. If they move, the speed is not constant: moving forwards means the machine is running too fast and moving backwards running too slow.

Sub-mixing (18) Mixing selected sources in separate groups. In a simple music recording for example some microphones may be assigned to one group for mixing separately before the output is mixed with other sources. This allows different treatment and control.

Syndication (130) Duplicated items—interviews and programmes—supplied to several stations.

Talkback (15–18, 36, 37) Instructions from control room to studio using the equivalent of an intercom.

Talk-over (82, 83) Speech made over music; also one person speaking at same time as another.

Tape feedback echo (152, 153) Artificial reverberation created by recording a signal and replaying it a fraction of a second later.

Taster/teaser (76) Short item or sequence at beginning of a programme of what is to come later.

Top (34) High frequencies.

Trailer (64, 65) Sequence advertising programmes; also uncoated tape used to mark the end of a recording.

Transducer (152, 153) Converts power from one form to another i.e. loudspeakers, microphones, pick-ups and tape heads.

UHF (100, 101) Ultra high frequency.

VHF (50, 100–104) Very high frequency. Frequency bands on which FM transmissions are made.

VU meter (32, 33) Volume unit meter. Used for measuring programme volume. Marked in percentage modulation.

Voice-over unit (18, 19, 30, 31, 77) Automatically reduces level in the presence of another signal e.g. from a microphone, allowing presenters and DJs to talk over music without manually reducing the level.

Voice piece (122) Single prepared items of speech on a particular theme or topic. Used extensively in news programmes.

Vox pop, vox populi (94, 95) The people's voice. A series of comments or reactions edited together to form a general opinion.

Wheel (75) The chart a presenter works to showing a rough sequence of items in a programme. Also called a *clock*.

Windshield (93) Foam cover which helps reduce wind noise when a microphone is used outdoors. Used indoors it can help reduce *popping* and breath sounds when a microphone is held too close to the mouth.

Wow-in (70) Sound created when records and tapes are played without allowing the correct run up to full speed before the beginning.